MW00682803

CONSTRUCTION LICENSE

as original purchaser of plan number

Is hereby granted a non-transferable, non-exclusive license to build the home depicted in this plan and is given the right to reproduce this plan only as required for such construction. No re-use fee is required if the original purchaser builds this home more than once. Permission is also given to make modifications to this plan, but no permission is given to claim copyright on the original or any derivative works of this plan. No other rights are granted and any further distribution is strictly prohibited.

Signed

Date

License Number

Valid when the official Gold Seal™ is embossed above.

RETAIN IN YOUR FILES FOR FUTURE REFERENCE

design basics inc.
HOME PLAN DESIGN SERVICE

11112 John Galt Boulevard   Omaha, Nebraska 68137
Toll Free 800-947-PLAN
402-331-9223   FAX 402-331-5507

You get more than just a set of construction drawings . . .

You receive a construction license that grants you, the purchaser, the right to build the home as many times as you wish, with no re-use fee. You also receive the right to make modifications to vellum copies of the original design and the right to make blueprints from vellum copies for construction purposes only. For more details see the example construction license at left.

More Importantly . . .

When you purchase one of our home plans, you tap into the design expertise that has made Design Basics the largest home plan design firm in the nation.

If you've ever paid to have a home plan designed from scratch, you know it's expensive – and time consuming. We invest thousands of dollars and a vast amount of time to painstakingly develop each one of our home plans. But because of our plan service approach, we can offer our award-winning designs for only a fraction of the cost. Plus, you'll have them within two business days.

FOR YOUR PROTECTION

To discourage illegal usage of our home plans, and to help protect your rights as the legal holder of a Design Basics construction license, the symbol shown below now appears on all of our construction drawings. It is a reminder to all, that as the purchaser of a Design Basics home plan, you have specific legal rights that need to be protected.

Design Basics Copyright facts to remember.

Every home plan (as well as the artists' renderings of every home plan) featured in this publication has been registered with the U.S. Copyright Office by Design Basics Inc.

When you purchase a Design Basics home plan, you receive a validated construction license. The construction license gives the purchaser legal rights, including the right to build the plan as many times as desired and to modify the construction drawings in connection with that construction.

If you make modifications to a Design Basics home plan, including the artist's rendering of that home plan, the rights to use of the modified plan and the right to claim of copyright in the modified plan are still governed by Design Basics as owner of the copyright on the original home plan. NOTE – Regardless of how extensive the changes are, no claim to copyright may be made in any modified Design Basics home plan.

ALL DESIGN BASICS PLANS HAVE BEEN REGISTERED

ORIGINAL

DRAFT

WITH THE U.S. COPYRIGHT OFFICE

Redrawing and/or constructing a home that utilizes design elements, either in whole or in part, based on a copyrighted Design Basics home plan, without first obtaining a valid Design Basics construction license constitutes infringement of U.S. copyright law and can carry penalties of up to $100,000 per violation.

With your purchase of a Design Basics plan, you also receive a copyright release for our artwork. This gives you our permission to use our rendered elevation and floor plan(s) of the design in your promotional materials. However, Design Basics' name and copyright must appear along with the rendered artwork.

THE ABOVE POINTS ARE PROVIDED AS GENERAL GUIDELINES ONLY.

TO OUR VALUED CUSTOMERS

Within these pages may lie someone's dream. Another's lifetime investment. And for you, perhaps the opportunity for individual achievement and creative expression. This is our latest **Gold Seal**™ **Home Plan** Collection, specifically developed for you and your home buyers. From the time each of these designs were conceptualized to the moment the last line was drawn, we, at Design Basics, have kept in mind the fact that *your* execution of our designs brings to life our mission – to create the dreams that will bring your buyers "home."

You may understand by now that "Bringing People Home" is our mission. But what does that really mean for you? "Bringing People Home" is a pledge that all of our products and services are developed with the commitment to help you give your buyers their dreams of home. Gold Seal™ is an integral part of that, providing 442 distinct and spirited designs rooted in the basics: well-balanced elevations and logical, livable floor plans. They are designs that have been carefully reviewed for structural soundness and buildability. Designs with an intangible appeal, that when built, only your buyers can choose as the place to call home.

Part of our mission too, means designing the **Gold Seal**™ **Home Plan** Collection to be the easiest, most logical plan book available. This five-volume set is encyclopedically organized so you and your buyers can quickly and effortlessly find the ideal home. We created **Homes of Sophistication** – 106 diverse, comfortable floor plans between 1800' - 2199' – in an effort to help you bring your customers a little closer to home. Page by page. Design by design. And dream by dream.

HOME PLANS

Timeless quality and precise detail are combined to provide home plans designed with attention to today's buyer and practicality for today's builder.

SERVICE INFORMATION

Gold Seal™ Home Plans
Homes of Sophistication is published by
Design Basics Inc.
11112 John Galt Boulevard
Omaha, NE 68137-2384
Text and design copyright © 1996
by Design Basics Inc.

· INDEX ·

RANCH
HOMES

PRICE CODE
GS3006-18 Grayson

▶ High quality, erasable, reproducible vellums
▶ Shipped via 2nd day air within the continental U.S.

- beautiful columns and arched transoms are focal points of this ranch home elevation
- 10-foot entry has formal views of volume dining room and great room featuring brick fireplace and arched windows

- large island kitchen offers angled range and pantry
- sunny breakfast room has atrium door to back yard
- garage with built-in shelves accesses home through efficient laundry room

- separate bedroom wings provide optimum privacy
- private master suite includes whirlpool bath with sloped ceiling, plant shelf above dual lavs and large walk-in closet

Rear Elevation

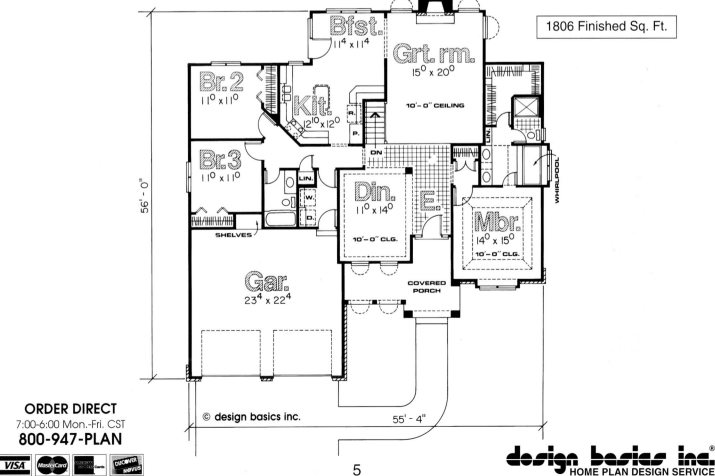

1806 Finished Sq. Ft.

© design basics inc.

design basics inc.®
HOME PLAN DESIGN SERVICE

PRICE CODE
GS1559-18 Bancroft

▶ **High quality, erasable, reproducible vellums**
▶ **Shipped via 2nd day air within the continental U.S.**

- front porch features repeating arches
- hard-surfaced traffic ways
- 10-foot ceilings through entry, great room and staircase
- sunny dinette with planning desk and bayed window

- roomy kitchen with pantry, 2 lazy Susans and snack bar shares see-thru fireplace with great room
- wet bar/servery between dinette and great room
- oversized garage with plenty of storage

- volume master bedroom with arched window
- master bath has walk-in closet, his and her vanities and corner whirlpool tub with windows above
- Hollywood bath for secondary bedrooms

Rear Elevation

Parade Home Package
available for all plans

1808 Finished Sq. Ft.

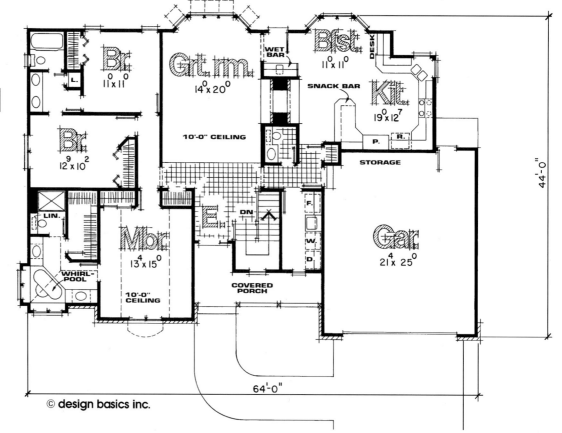

ORDER DIRECT
7:00-6:00 Mon.-Fri. CST
800-947-PLAN

© design basics inc.

design basics inc.
HOME PLAN DESIGN SERVICE

PRICE CODE

GS2461-18 Shawnee

▶ **High quality, erasable, reproducible vellums**
▶ **Shipped via 2nd day air within the continental U.S.**

Gold Seal
HOME PLANS™

- appealing roofline and covered porch with repeating arches
- kitchen/dinette area includes bayed eating area, wrapping counters, desk, island and wet bar/servery for entertaining ease

- impactful 10-foot-high entry
- decorative hutch space in dining room
- windows frame fireplace in great room
- laundry/mud room with sink and extra counter space

- bedroom #2 can be utilized as an optional den
- master suite enjoys decorative boxed ceiling and elegant windows to the rear, dual lavs, walk-in closet, whirlpool and cedar-lined window seat for storage

Rear Elevation

1850 Finished Sq. Ft.

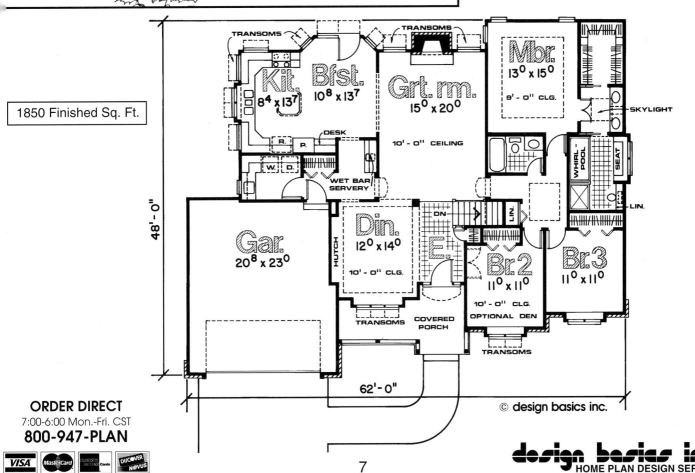

ORDER DIRECT
7:00-6:00 Mon.-Fri. CST
800-947-PLAN

VISA MasterCard American Express Cards DISCOVER NOVUS

© design basics inc.

design basics inc.®
HOME PLAN DESIGN SERVICE

PRICE CODE
GS3299-18 Tatum

▶ High quality, erasable, reproducible vellums
▶ Shipped via 2nd day air within the continental U.S.

- generous 11'-11" ceiling in great room invites guests inside to warm by its fireplace
- gourmet kitchen with cooktop in island
- dining room has views to the back through picturesque windows

- breakfast area with planning desk connects kitchen and dining room
- back porch is great place to relax
- secluded bedroom wing
- arched opening unveils boxed 9-foot ceiling in master bedroom

- French doors add elegance to master bath equipped with leisurely whirlpool tub and double vanity
- two secondary bedrooms share hall bath

Rear Elevation

Version of GS3298-17 the "Ogden" as seen on page 46 of Homes of Distinction.

ALL PLANS *Customizable*

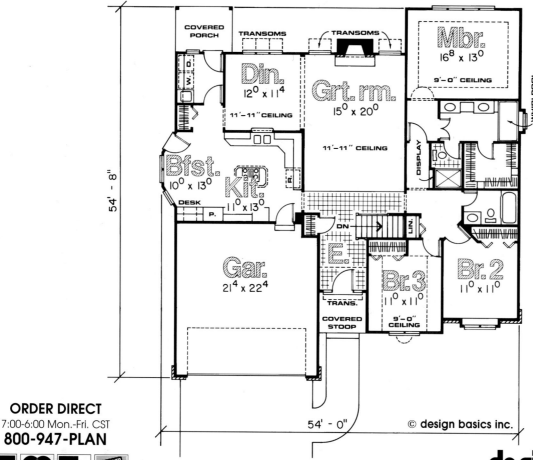

1873 Finished Sq. Ft.

54' - 8"

54' - 0"

© design basics inc.

ORDER DIRECT
7:00-6:00 Mon.-Fri. CST
800-947-PLAN

VISA MasterCard AMERICAN EXPRESS DISCOVER NOVUS

design basics inc.
HOME PLAN DESIGN SERVICE

PRICE CODE

GS2799-18 Hawthorne

▶ High quality, erasable, reproducible vellums
▶ Shipped via 2nd day air within the continental U.S.

- majesty window highlights handsome brick front elevation
- bowed windows and high ceiling provide terrific airy feeling to great room
- large laundry accessible from kitchen and garage

- family living is highlighted in integrated design of gathering room, spacious dinette and kitchen, all with special ceiling treatments
- gathering room boasts built-in entertainment center and 2 bookcases

- double doors into master dressing area featuring angled lavs, make-up counter and huge walk-in closet with cedar chest
- optional finished basement designed for independent living, with kitchen, bath and private access

Rear Elevation

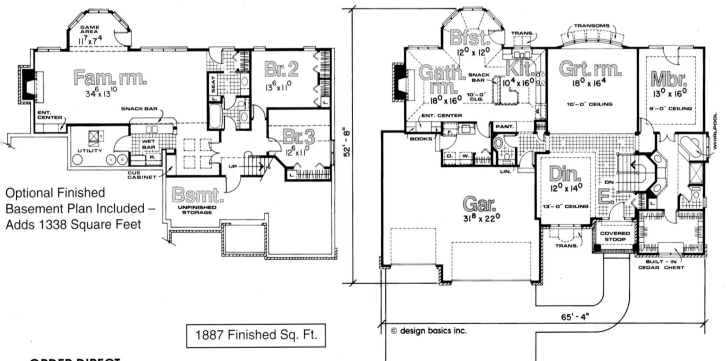

Optional Finished
Basement Plan Included –
Adds 1338 Square Feet

1887 Finished Sq. Ft.

© design basics inc.

ORDER DIRECT

7:00-6:00 Mon.-Fri. CST

800-947-PLAN

9

PRICE CODE

GS1748-19 Sinclair

Gold Seal
HOME PLANS™

▸ **High quality, erasable, reproducible vellums**
▸ **Shipped via 2nd day air within the continental U.S.**

- alternate elevation at no extra cost
- 10-foot ceiling at entry and great room
- beautiful arched dining room window and detailed ceiling to 12 foot high
- see-thru fireplace seen from entry
- hearth area open to kitchen

- gourmet kitchen caters to the serious cook with corner sink, pantry, snack bar and adjacent eating area
- add French doors to bedroom adjacent to great room for optional den, remove closet for built-in bookcase

- master bedroom with vaulted ceiling and corner windows
- complete master bath area with skylight, whirlpool, his and her vanity and large walk-in closet

Rear Elevation

Alternate Elevation At No Extra Cost

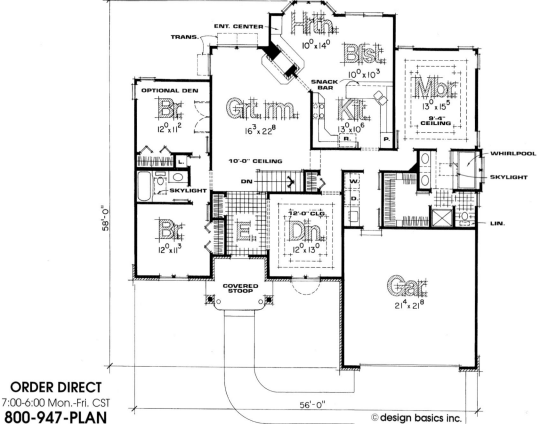

1911 Finished Sq. Ft.

ORDER DIRECT
7:00-6:00 Mon.-Fri. CST
800-947-PLAN

VISA   MasterCard   Cards   DISCOVER NOVUS

© design basics inc.

design basics inc
HOME PLAN DESIGN SERVICE

PRICE CODE

GS2384-19 Surrey

▶ High quality, erasable, reproducible vellums
▶ Shipped via 2nd day air within the continental U.S.

Gold Seal
HOME PLANS

- wood and brick details and elegant porch highlight elevation
- entry with 10-foot ceiling views open dining room with tapered columns
- gourmet kitchen includes island, pantry and wrapping wet bar/servery

- sunny bayed dinette with outdoor access
- great room enjoys a warm fireplace flanked by large windows with arched transoms above
- comfortable secondary bedrooms share cozy Hollywood bath with linen cabinet

- elegant master suite enjoys vaulted ceilings, pampering master bath with his and her vanities, whirlpool, linen cabinet, special shower and roomy walk-in closet
- garage includes extra storage space and door to side yard

Rear Elevation

ALL PLANS *Customizable*

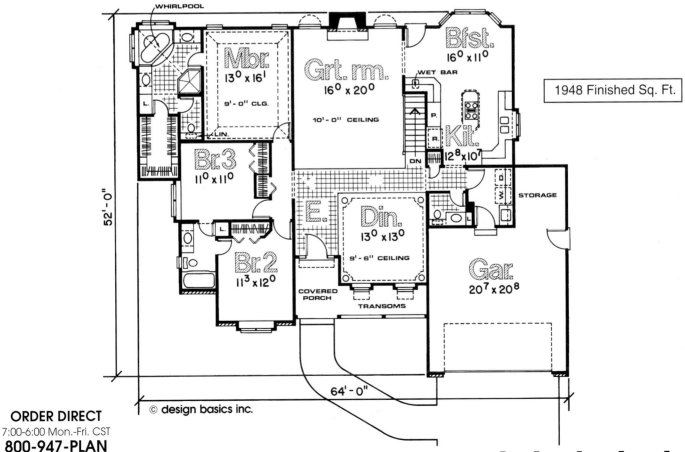

1948 Finished Sq. Ft.

© design basics inc.

ORDER DIRECT
7:00-6:00 Mon.-Fri. CST
800-947-PLAN

design basics inc.
HOME PLAN DESIGN SERVICE

GS3553-19 Glenmorrie

PRICE CODE

- angled garage adds interest to elevation
- dining room displays elegance of 10'-0" ceiling
- volume great room offers plenty of space and light for gathering

- oak kitchen and breakfast area provide peninsula snack bar and bayed windows
- hearth room off the kitchen highlighted with warm fireplace between glass
- secluded bedroom wing
- master bedroom boasts boxed ceiling

- walk-in closet and whirlpool under sloped ceiling are features in master suite
- secondary bedrooms utilize convenient hall bath
- corner closet in roomy laundry

Rear Elevation

Parade Home Package

available for all plans

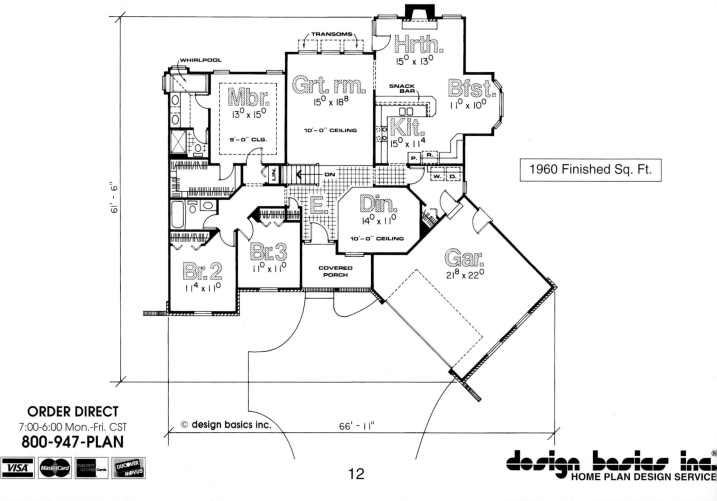

1960 Finished Sq. Ft.

© design basics inc.

design basics inc.
HOME PLAN DESIGN SERVICE

GS3276-**19** Cedardale

PRICE CODE

▶ High quality, erasable, reproducible vellums
▶ Shipped via 2nd day air within the continental U.S.

- arched details and covered porch invite further inspection of this ranch style home
- formal dining is enhanced by oak floor, ceiling detail and hutch space
- dramatic stairs with dome ceiling above are unique features
- island with cooktop range, roomy pantry and desk highlight kitchen/dinette area
- family room has inviting brick fireplace and spacious windows to back
- volume ceiling and arched transom window compliment master bedroom
- master bath includes 10'-4" ceiling, oval whirlpool tub and walk-in closet
- bedrooms #2 and #3 share convenient hall bath
- laundry room is located close to bedrooms and offers sunny window

Rear Elevation

1973 Finished Sq. Ft.

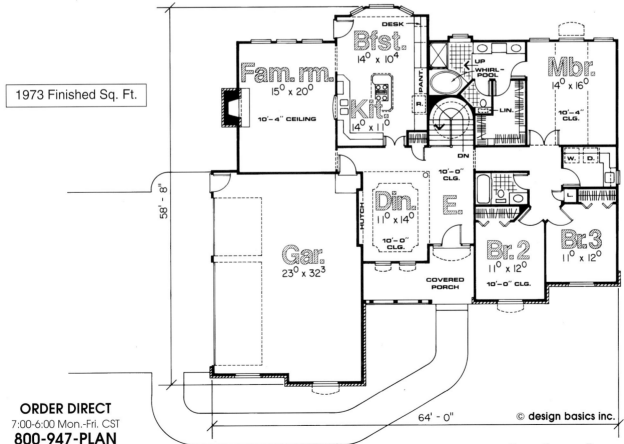

© design basics inc.

ORDER DIRECT
7:00-6:00 Mon.-Fri. CST

800-947-PLAN

HOME PLAN DESIGN SERVICE

GS3031-19 Jonesville

PRICE CODE

Gold Seal
HOME PLANS™

- special detailing and front porch create sophisticated elevation
- dramatic formal dining room open to 10-foot-tall entry
- living room has large windows and cased opening to family room

- family room open to kitchen and breakfast area provides great atmosphere for informal gatherings
- breakfast area with 2 pantries and built-in desk complements island kitchen
- laundry has access to covered porch

- secondary bedrooms off entry share hall bath
- French doors open to master suite, enhanced by private back yard access and whirlpool bath with spacious closet and dual lavs

Rear Elevation

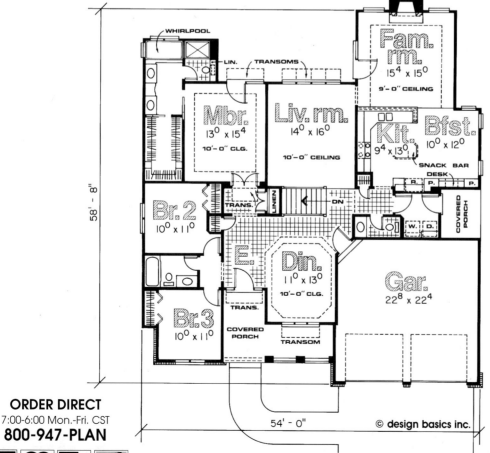

1978 Finished Sq. Ft.

58' - 8"

54' - 0"

© design basics inc.

design basics inc.®
HOME PLAN DESIGN SERVICE

PRICE CODE

GS1539-19 Mansfield

Gold Seal
HOME PLANS

- hard surface trafficways
- formal dining room with hutch space and tiered ceiling up to 11-foot-high
- combination mud/laundry room for easy access from garage
- tandem 3-car drive-through garage

- efficient kitchen with snack bar and planning desk
- sunny bayed breakfast area
- gorgeous fireplace surrounded by windows in great room with built-in bookcase and 10-foot ceiling

- skylit master bath with whirlpool, his and her vanities and plant ledge
- his and her walk-in closets
- living room with volume ceiling can become third bedroom

Rear Elevation

Parade
Home
Package
available for all plans

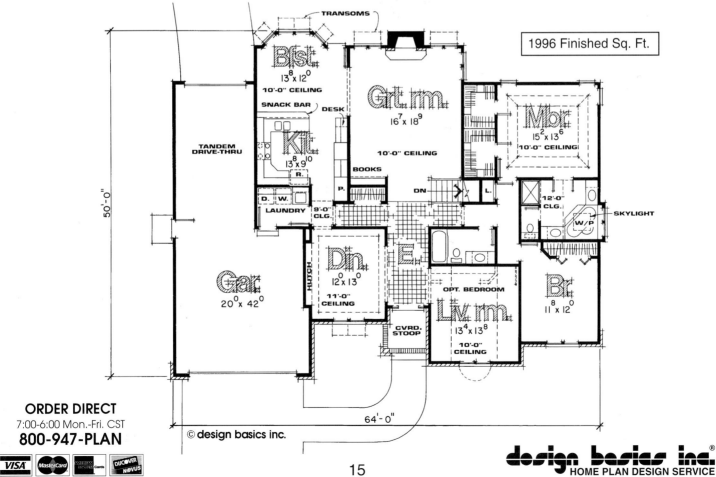

1996 Finished Sq. Ft.

ORDER DIRECT
7:00-6:00 Mon.-Fri. CST
800-947-PLAN

VISA MasterCard AMERICAN EXPRESS Cards DISCOVER NOVUS

© design basics inc.

design basics inc.®
HOME PLAN DESIGN SERVICE

PRICE CODE

GS2361-20 Summerwood

Gold Seal HOME PLANS™

▶ High quality, erasable, reproducible vellums
▶ Shipped via 2nd day air within the continental U.S.

- elegant covered porch with arch above door adds romantic appeal to elevation
- formal dining room viewed from entry
- assets in ideal great room include 3-sided see-thru fireplace, entertainment center and bookcases

- bay windowed hearth room with 10-foot ceiling and see-thru fireplace offers a cozy retreat
- kitchen and dinette designed for livability with snack bar, pantry and ample counter space

- window seat framed by closets enhances bedroom #2; bedroom #3 can be converted to an optional den
- private master suite enjoys boxed ceiling, skylit dressing area with his and her lavs, corner whirlpool and large walk-in closet

Rear Elevation

PROMOTIONAL LICENSE

Black and White, Camera-Ready Artwork of the home plan FREE with any plan purchase to assist you in advertising the home.

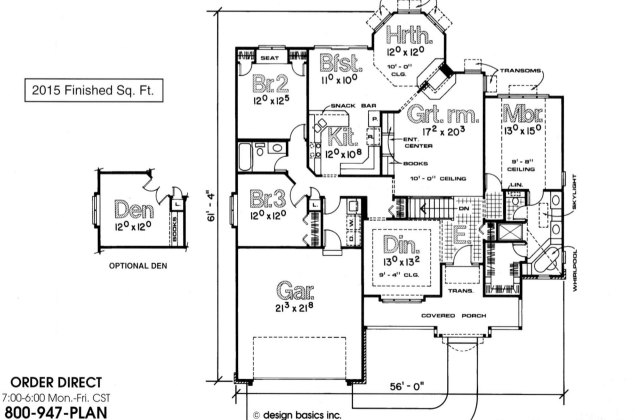

2015 Finished Sq. Ft.

OPTIONAL DEN

56' - 0"

© design basics inc.

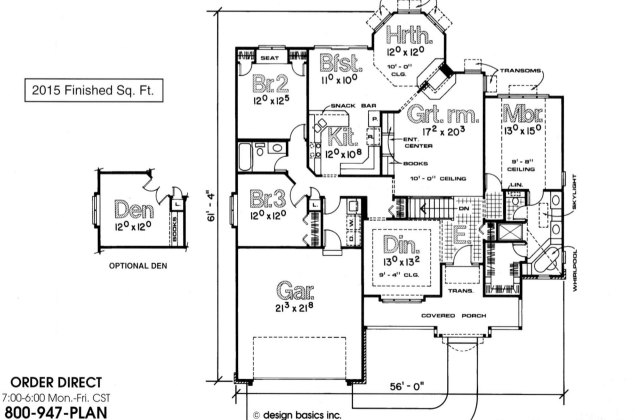

design basics inc
HOME PLAN DESIGN SERVICE

PRICE CODE

GS2843-20 Atwood

▶ High quality, erasable, reproducible vellums
▶ Shipped via 2nd day air within the continental U.S.

- handsome ranch home features wood railing on lovely covered porch
- plan allows private den off entry to be converted to optional third bedroom
- dining room has 10-foot ceiling with space for buffet or hutch

- oak flooring in entry and hall to dinette
- tall windows grace fireplace, and 10-foot ceiling adds sophistcation to great room
- beautiful French doors open to airy dinette/kitchen area with access to outside

- accessed by French doors, the master bedroom features generous walk-in closet
- 2nd set of French doors open to master bath with dual lavs, whirlpool and shower with seat
- bedroom #2 enjoys volume ceiling

Rear Elevation

ALL PLANS Customizable

2047 Finished Sq. Ft.

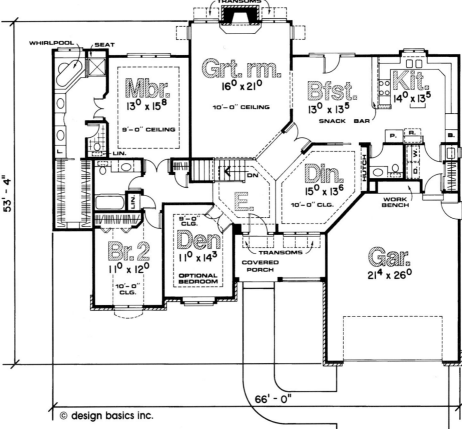

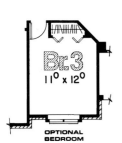

ORDER DIRECT
7:00-6:00 Mon.-Fri. CST
800-947-PLAN

© design basics inc.

design basics inc®
HOME PLAN DESIGN SERVICE

GS3139-20 Foxboro

PRICE CODE

▶ High quality, erasable, reproducible vellums
▶ Shipped via 2nd day air within the continental U.S.

Gold Seal™
HOME PLANS

- universally designed home
- arched details decorate this quaint ranch style home
- formal entry presents great room with brick fireplace, transoms and 10-foot-high ceiling

- sizeable breakfast area shines with bayed windows and access to screen porch
- spacious peninsula kitchen contains snack bar, pantry and pull-out shelf for extra counter space

- master suite features bayed window, roomy closet, dressing area, dual lavs, whirlpool bath and oversized shower
- bedroom #3 has window seat, 9-foot-high ceiling and can be an optional den
- stairs to basement have elevator option

Rear Elevation

Parade Home Package
available for all plans

2053 Finished Sq. Ft.

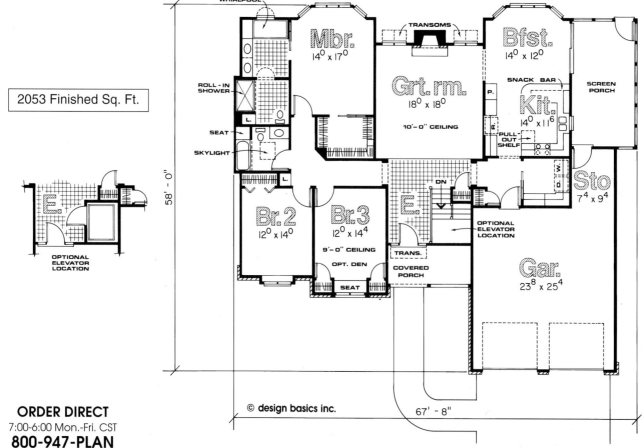

© design basics inc.

OPTIONAL ELEVATOR LOCATION

ORDER DIRECT
7:00-6:00 Mon.-Fri. CST
800-947-PLAN

18

design basics inc.
HOME PLAN DESIGN SERVICE

GS2222-20 Plainview

PRICE CODE **20**

Gold Seal
HOME PLANS

▸ High quality, erasable, reproducible vellums
▸ Shipped via 2nd day air within the continental U.S.

- elegant covered veranda at entry
- 10-foot or higher ceilings in entry and great room
- spectacular window out the back highlights great room
- 3-sided fireplace serves gathering areas

- abundance of windows throughout
- pantry, planning desk, and island counter with snack bar in kitchen
- convenient powder bath location
- garage with extra storage space accesses home through laundry/mud room

- den becomes third bedroom with optional door location
- irresistible master suite with private covered deck and pampering dressing area with whirlpool and large walk-in closet

Rear Elevation

2068 Finished Sq. Ft.

ORDER DIRECT

7:00-6:00 Mon.-Fri. CST

800-947-PLAN

© design basics inc.

design basics inc®
HOME PLAN DESIGN SERVICE

GS3303-20 Richardson

▶ **High quality, erasable, reproducible vellums**
▶ **Shipped via 2nd day air within the continental U.S.**

- brick accents, hip roofs and an arched entry compliment this quaint ranch home
- entry reveals formal dining with 11'-0" high ceiling, transom windows and hutch space
- gourmet kitchen features wrapping cabinets, island, double oven and pantry

- hearth room with entertainment center shares 3-sided fireplace with great room
- transom windows showcased under volume ceiling in the great room
- master suite is highlighted by vaulted ceiling with French doors to bath area

- master bath contains his and her vanities, whirlpool tub and spacious walk-in closet
- 9'-0" main level walls
- optional finished basement plan shows secondary bedrooms, informal living area and plenty of storage

Rear Elevation

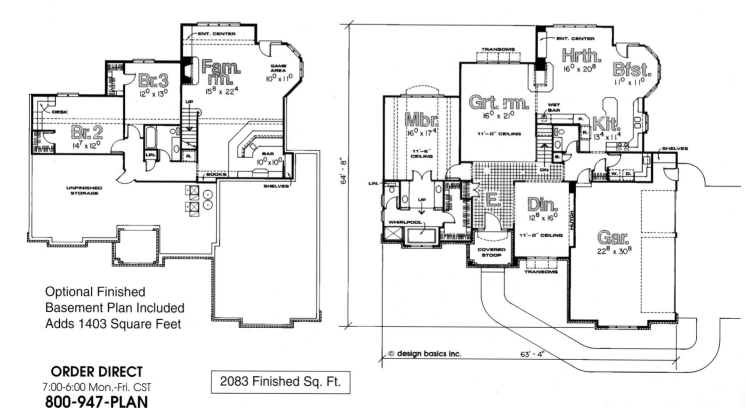

Optional Finished
Basement Plan Included
Adds 1403 Square Feet

2083 Finished Sq. Ft.

ORDER DIRECT
7:00-6:00 Mon.-Fri. CST
800-947-PLAN

HOME PLAN DESIGN SERVICE

GS2454-20 Pickford

Gold Seal™
HOME PLANS

▶ **High quality, erasable, reproducible vellums**
▶ **Shipped via 2nd day air within the continental U.S.**

- elevation has eye-catching curb appeal
- 10-foot ceiling in spacious great room with raised hearth fireplace and two windows with arched transoms above
- French doors off great room access den with spider-beamed ceiling

- formal dining room close to great room and kitchen area affords entertaining ease
- island kitchen and bayed dinette with outside access features desk, pantry and lazy Susan

- comfortable secondary bedrooms are apart from private master suite
- master suite enhancements include boxed ceiling, walk-in closet, his and her vanities with knee space and whirlpool tub

Rear Elevation

ORIGINAL © DRAFT

ALL DESIGN BASICS PLANS HAVE BEEN REGISTERED WITH THE U.S. COPYRIGHT OFFICE

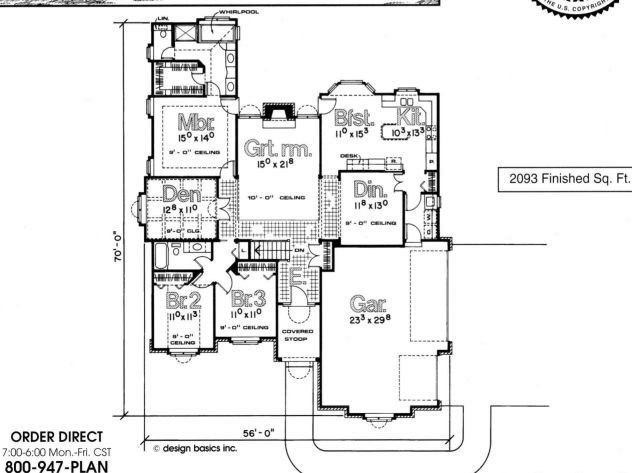

2093 Finished Sq. Ft.

ORDER DIRECT
7:00-6:00 Mon.-Fri. CST

800-947-PLAN

VISA MasterCard American Express Cards Discover NOVUS

© design basics inc.

design basics inc.®
HOME PLAN DESIGN SERVICE

GS3196-21 Galloway

PRICE CODE

▶ **High quality, erasable, reproducible vellums**
▶ **Shipped via 2nd day air within the continental U.S.**

- stucco and brick details complement this ranch style home
- ceiling details enhance formal dining room
- formal living room has view of screen porch through spacious windows

- family room is warmed by fireplace and provides access to screen porch
- breakfast/kitchen area boasts broom closet, snack bar, pantry and lazy Susans

- master suite features large walk-in closet, dual lavs and whirlpool bath
- secondary bedrooms share convenient hall bath

Rear Elevation

PROMOTIONAL LICENSE
Black and White, Camera-Ready Artwork of the home plan FREE with any plan purchase to assist you in advertising the home.

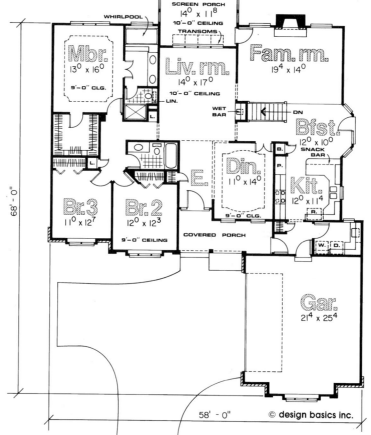

2120 Finished Sq. Ft.

ORDER DIRECT
7:00-6:00 Mon.-Fri. CST
800-947-PLAN

© design basics inc.

design basics inc.
HOME PLAN DESIGN SERVICE

22

GS3597-PRICE CODE 21 Concorde

▶ **High quality, erasable, reproducible vellums**
▶ **Shipped via 2nd day air within the continental U.S.**

- unique front porch has charming appeal
- oak entry views elegant living room with French doors to covered patio
- 10'-0" ceiling and bowed windows compliment dining room

- kitchen is wrapped in counters and features snack bar
- breakfast area brightened with bayed windows
- raised hearth fireplace warms secluded family room

- sunny whirlpool and walk-in closet complete master suite
- secondary bedrooms in secluded wing afford privacy for master suite
- covered patio enhanced with tapered columns

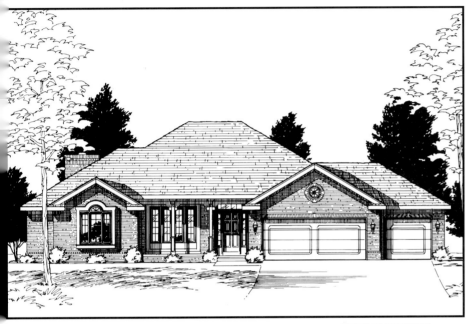

Rear Elevation

2132 Finished Sq. Ft.

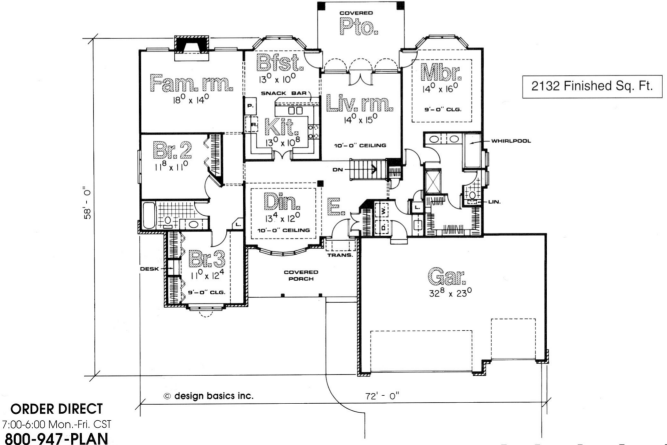

ORDER DIRECT
7:00-6:00 Mon.-Fri. CST
800-947-PLAN

design basics inc.®
HOME PLAN DESIGN SERVICE

GS1689-21 Newman

▶ **High quality, erasable, reproducible vellums**
▶ **Shipped via 2nd day air within the continental U.S.**

- many lot arrangement possibilities
- visually open plan
- diagonal views give expansive look
- arched ceiling at entry
- entry views volume great room with fireplace flanked by windows

- stunning dining room
- island kitchen with snack bar, desk and walk-in pantry adjoins bayed breakfast area
- 3-car garage with extra storage space accesses home through mud/laundry room

- secondary bedrooms share hall bath
- double doors lead to master bedroom with tiered ceiling and access to covered deck
- romantic master bath with whirlpool, double vanity and walk-in closet

Rear Elevation

Parade Home Package
available for all plans

2133 Finished Sq. Ft.

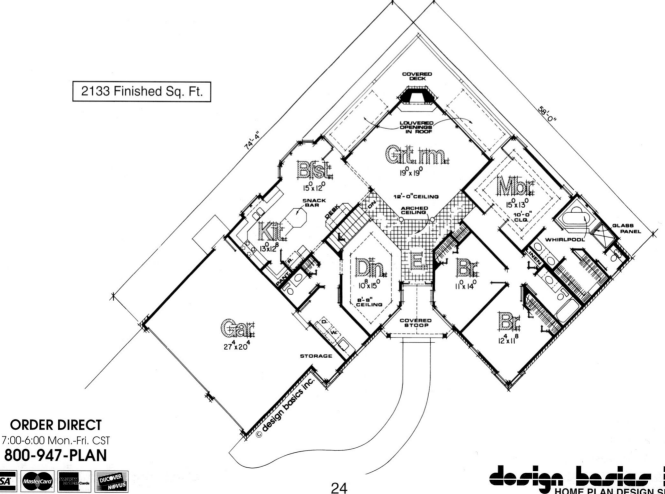

PRICE CODE
GS3145-**21** Gregory

▶ **High quality, erasable, reproducible vellums**
▶ **Shipped via 2nd day air within the continental U.S.**

- covered porch with arched detailing creates a charming elevation to this ranch style home
- formal entry views great room and dining room with 10'-4" ceilings

- angled breakfast area with octagon ceiling detail is accessible to kitchen and dining room
- peninsula kitchen features snack bar, 2 pantries and buffet
- French doors open to private den

- cathedral ceiling opens up the master bedroom
- separate dressing area, whirlpool bath and walk-in closet complement this master suite
- extra storage space or workshop area in garage

Rear Elevation

PROMOTIONAL LICENSE

Black and White, Camera-Ready Artwork of the home plan FREE with any plan purchase to assist you in advertising the home.

2141 Finished Sq. Ft.

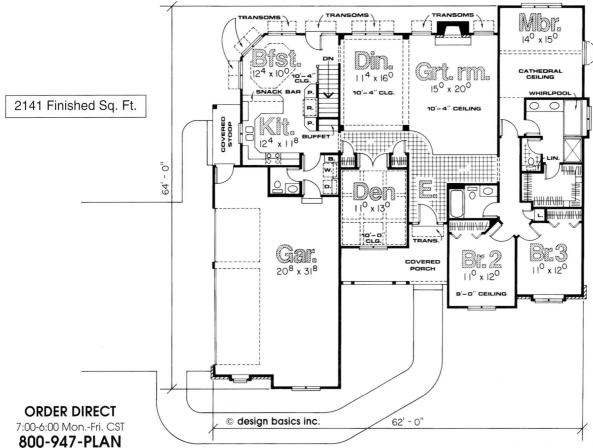

© design basics inc.

ORDER DIRECT
7:00-6:00 Mon.-Fri. CST
800-947-PLAN

PRICE CODE

GS2848-21 Roxbury

▶ High quality, erasable, reproducible vellums
▶ Shipped via 2nd day air within the continental U.S.

Gold Seal HOME PLANS™

- tasteful full brick front elevation highlighted by striking windows
- long views through great room create sense of spaciousness
- formal dining room with hutch space and 12-foot-high ceiling

- garage offers extra storage space
- window over utility sink in laundry
- well-appointed island kitchen includes 42" pantry, planning desk and snack bar
- see-thru fireplace serves kitchen, breakfast area, and volume great room

- front bedroom with window seat, 10-foot ceiling and pocket door to bath easily converts to den by adding double doors
- built-in bookcase in den
- private master suite includes sterling bath area with plant shelf and step-up whirlpool

Rear Elevation

ORIGINAL **C** DRAFT
ALL DESIGN BASICS PLANS HAVE BEEN REGISTERED WITH THE U.S. COPYRIGHT OFFICE

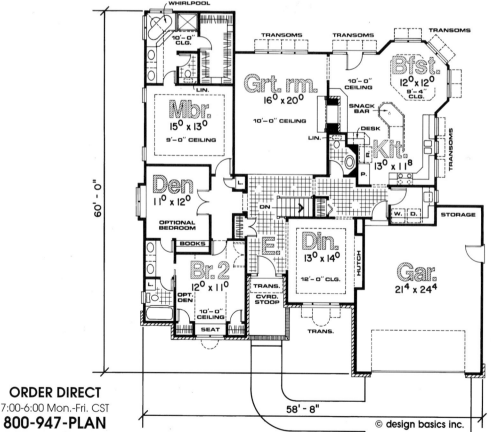

2148 Finished Sq. Ft.

ORDER DIRECT

7:00-6:00 Mon.-Fri. CST

800-947-PLAN

VISA · MasterCard · AMERICAN EXPRESS Cards · DISCOVER NOVUS

© design basics inc.

26

design basics inc®
HOME PLAN DESIGN SERVICE

GS2213-21 Essex

PRICE CODE **21**

▶ High quality, erasable, reproducible vellums
▶ Shipped via 2nd day air within the continental U.S.

- open entry views formal rooms
- volume ceilings in major living spaces
- comfortable family room with spider-beamed ceiling and fireplace
- service doors to close off kitchen from entry and dining room

- built-in desk, snack bar and pantry in kitchen
- open staircase for future finished basement
- French doors will turn bedroom #3 into den if desired

- compartmented Hollywood bath for secondary bedrooms
- private master suite with walk-in closet, double vanity and whirlpool under windows

Rear Elevation

Parade Home Package *available for all plans*

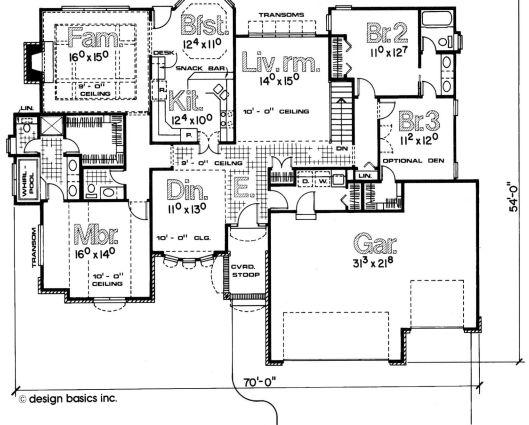

2149 Finished Sq. Ft.

© design basics inc.

ORDER DIRECT
7:00-6:00 Mon.-Fri. CST
800-947-PLAN

design basics inc.
HOME PLAN DESIGN SERVICE

GS2326-21 Greensboro

PRICE CODE

▶ High quality, erasable, reproducible vellums
▶ Shipped via 2nd day air within the continental U.S.

- appealing brick elevation
- formal living and dining rooms flanking entry give ease in entertaining
- impressive great room with 11-foot ceiling and picture/awning windows framing a raised hearth fireplace

- attractive kitchen/dinette area with island, desk, wrapping counters, walk-in pantry and access to covered patio
- 9-foot main level walls
- desirable 3-car side-load garage has extra storage space

- growing families or empty nesters have the option of converting two bedrooms to other uses
- pampering master suite enjoys skylit dressing area, walk-in closet, dual lavs, whirlpool tub and decorative plant shelf

Rear Elevation

Black and White, Camera-Ready Artwork of the home plan FREE with any plan purchase to assist you in advertising the home.

PROMOTIONAL LICENSE

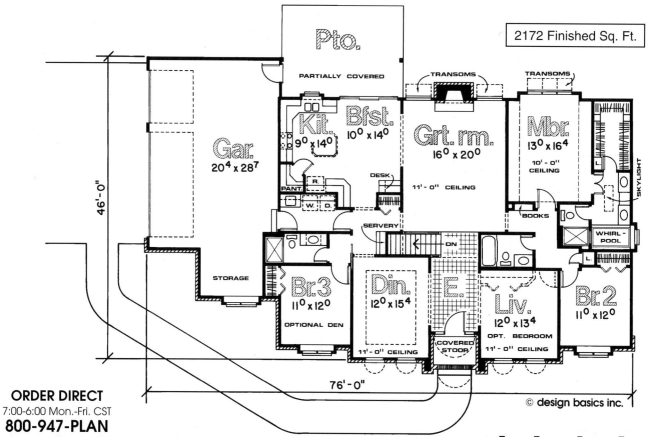

2172 Finished Sq. Ft.

Pto.
PARTIALLY COVERED

TRANSOMS   TRANSOMS

Gar.
20⁴ x 28⁷

Kit.
9⁰ x 14⁰

Bfst.
10⁰ x 14⁰

Grt. rm.
16⁰ x 20⁰
11'-0" CEILING

Mbr.
13⁰ x 16⁴
10'-0" CEILING

DESK

PANT.   R.
W. D.

SERVERY

BOOKS

WHIRL-POOL

SKYLIGHT

46'-0"

STORAGE

Br.3
11⁰ x 12⁰
OPTIONAL DEN

Din.
12⁰ x 15⁴
11'-0" CEILING

E.

COVERED STOOP

Liv.
12⁰ x 13⁴
OPT. BEDROOM
11'-0" CEILING

Br.2
11⁰ x 12⁰

76'-0"

© design basics inc.

ORDER DIRECT
7:00-6:00 Mon.-Fri. CST
800-947-PLAN

VISA   MasterCard   DISCOVER NOVUS

design basics inc.
HOME PLAN DESIGN SERVICE

GS3005-21 Wrenwood

PRICE CODE **21**

- ▶ High quality, erasable, reproducible vellums
- ▶ Shipped via 2nd day air within the continental U.S.

- brick columns and tall gabled entry create prominent elevation
- bright 12-foot-tall entry views large great room with entertainment center, brick fireplace and direct access to dining room and kitchen

- gourmet island kitchen with wet bar, wrapping pantry and snack bar is well-integrated with bayed breakfast area and dining room
- utility corridor has laundry room to one side and computer center to the other

- 3-car garage has sunlit shop area
- secondary bedrooms share large bath
- bedroom #3 offers versatile den option
- master suite has spacious walk-in closet, lavish whirlpool bath and 10-foot ceiling in bedroom

Rear Elevation

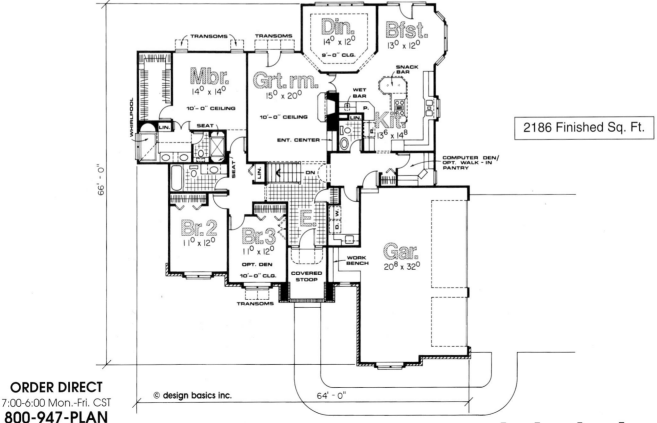

2186 Finished Sq. Ft.

ORDER DIRECT
7:00-6:00 Mon.-Fri. CST

800-947-PLAN

© design basics inc.

HOME PLAN DESIGN SERVICE

PRICE CODE
GS3598-21 Brentwood

▶ **High quality, erasable, reproducible vellums**
▶ **Shipped via 2nd day air within the continental U.S.**

- stucco accents front porch
- dining room has 10'-0" ceiling
- multiple arched windows accentuate impressive great room
- see-thru fireplace in hearth room

- snack bar and island counter equip kitchen and breakfast area
- French doors reveal master suite with walk-in closet, oval whirlpool and double sink vanity

- bedroom #2 easily converted to a den
- spacious laundry room with soaking sink and counter space
- 3-car side-load garage

Rear Elevation

Parade Home Package
available for all plans

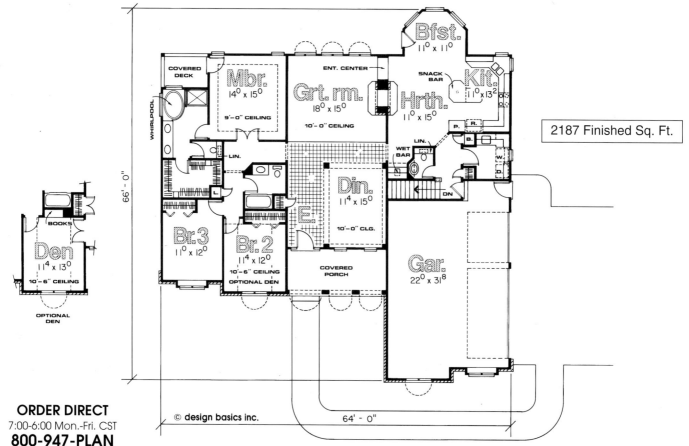

2187 Finished Sq. Ft.

ORDER DIRECT
7:00-6:00 Mon.-Fri. CST
800-947-PLAN

design basics inc.
HOME PLAN DESIGN SERVICE

PRICE CODE
GS3128-21 Alvarado

Gold Seal
HOME PLANS

▶ High quality, erasable, reproducible vellums
▶ Shipped via 2nd day air within the continental U.S.

- wrapping porch, with brick and stucco accents, provides unique elevation to ranch style home
- grand entry hall has views to formal dining room, great room and den with bedroom option

- bedroom #2 has built-in desk and large windows
- volume great room has fireplace and cased opening to breakfast area with back yard access

- curio cabinet and 2 pantries highlight peninsula kitchen
- master suite offers private covered porch, whirlpool bath with dual lavs, compartmented shower and mirrored doors to large walk-in closet

Rear Elevation

2199 Finished Sq. Ft.

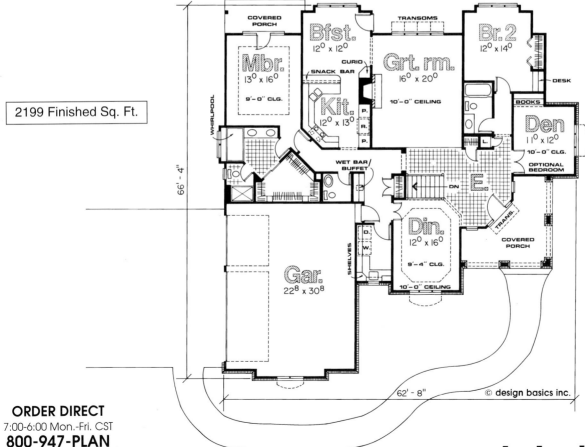

ORDER DIRECT
7:00-6:00 Mon.-Fri. CST
800-947-PLAN

design basics inc.®
HOME PLAN DESIGN SERVICE

1 ¹/₂ STORY HOMES

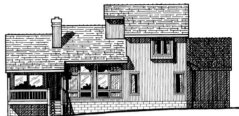

Gold Seal
HOME PLANS

▶ **High quality, erasable, reproducible vellums**
▶ **Shipped via 2nd day air within the continental U.S.**

- volume great room with large windows out the back
- see-thru fireplace between great room and dining room
- covered deck can easily become a screened-in porch

- efficient kitchen to the front with 2 lazy Susans and snack bar
- master bedroom on main level with clever bath arrangement which includes corner whirlpool tub with decorator ledge, iron-a-way and walk-in closet

- skylit staircase to second level
- hallway overlooking great room below
- upstairs convenient hall bath, clothes chute and 2 linen closets
- deep 3-car garage with extra storage space

Rear Elevation

ALL DESIGN BASICS PLANS HAVE BEEN REGISTERED
ORIGINAL
C
DRAFT
WITH THE U.S. COPYRIGHT OFFICE

© design basics inc.

Main	1229	Sq. Ft.
Second	600	Sq. Ft.
Total	1829	Sq. Ft.

ORDER DIRECT
7:00-6:00 Mon.-Fri. CST
800-947-PLAN

design basics inc.®
HOME PLAN DESIGN SERVICE

GS3065-18 Foster

PRICE CODE 18

Gold Seal
HOME PLANS™

▶ **High quality, erasable, reproducible vellums**
▶ **Shipped via 2nd day air within the continental U.S.**

- attractive 1½ story well suited for narrower lots
- U-stairs enhance entry with views of volume dining room and great room
- French doors to peninsula kitchen with 2 pantries and corner sink add drama

- breakfast area highlighted by boxed 10-foot-high ceiling, direct access to back yard and great room
- cathedral ceiling, arched windows and brick fireplace create a beautiful great room

- private master suite features 10-foot-high ceiling, whirlpool bath with open shower and generous walk-in closet
- upstairs secondary bedrooms, each with built-in desk, share large bath

Rear Elevation

Version of GS3075-20 the "Grant" as seen on page 52.

Parade Home Package
available for all plans

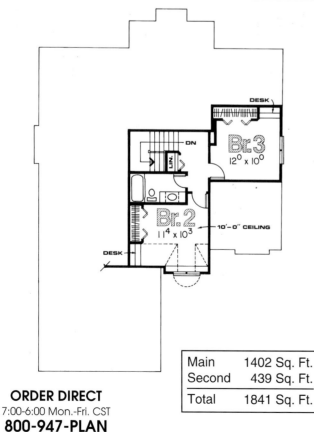

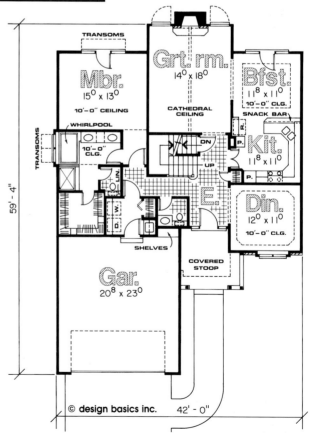

Main	1402 Sq. Ft.
Second	439 Sq. Ft.
Total	**1841 Sq. Ft.**

ORDER DIRECT
7:00-6:00 Mon.-Fri. CST
800-947-PLAN

VISA   MasterCard   American Express Cards   DISCOVER NOVUS

© design basics inc.

design basics inc.®
HOME PLAN DESIGN SERVICE

34

GS2569-18 Ohern

PRICE CODE

- eye-catching design is highlighted with brick accents and a large covered stoop distinguished by handsome wood columns
- spacious entry offers view of the great room with its grand 10'-8" ceiling and dramatic use of windows
- 10-foot-high ceilings give a distinctive personality to the thoughtfully planned kitchen and spacious dinette
- laundry area serves as mud entry from garage
- secluded from the traffic flow, the master suite offers privacy
- luxurious master bath features dual lavs, whirlpool, compartmented stool and walk-in closet

Gold Seal ™
HOME PLANS

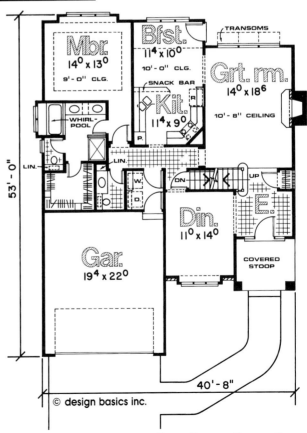

Rear Elevation

Version of GS2578-16 the "Kaiser" as seen on page 54 of Homes of Distinction.

PROMOTIONAL LICENSE • PROMOTIONAL LICENSE •
Black and White, Camera-Ready Artwork of the home plan FREE with any plan purchase to assist you in advertising the home.

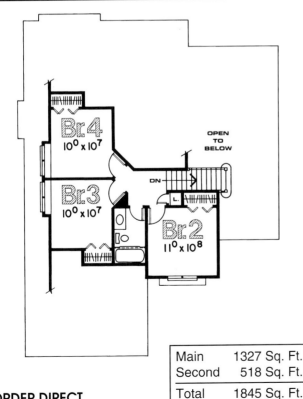

Main	1327 Sq. Ft.
Second	518 Sq. Ft.
Total	1845 Sq. Ft.

ORDER DIRECT
7:00-6:00 Mon.-Fri. CST

800-947-PLAN

© design basics inc.

design basics inc ®
HOME PLAN DESIGN SERVICE

35

GS2236-18 Bermier

PRICE CODE

▸ High quality, erasable, reproducible vellums
▸ Shipped via 2nd day air within the continental U.S.

- inviting covered front porch
- formal dining room with large boxed window seen from entry
- views into great room reveal handsome fireplace and tall windows

- snack bar, pantry, 2 lazy Susans and desk for kitchen/dinette area
- closet at service entry through garage
- window in laundry room
- large boxed window in volume master bedroom

- skylit master dressing area with double vanity, whirlpool, compartmented stool and shower
- upstairs, fourth bedroom has volume ceiling above beautiful arched window

Rear Elevation

Version of GS2245-16 the "Tyndale" as seen on page 55 of Homes of Distinction.

ALL PLANS *Customizable*

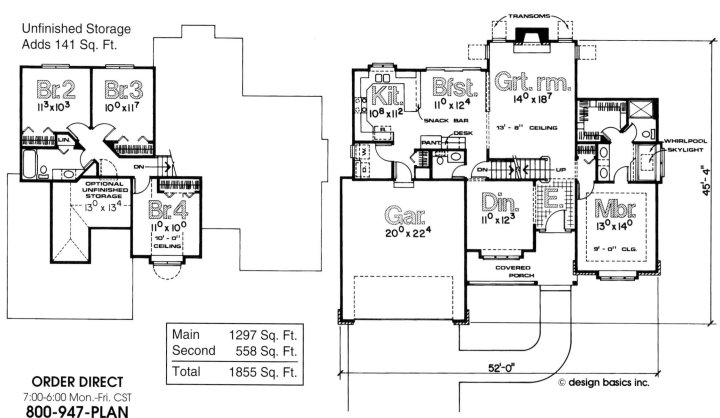

Unfinished Storage Adds 141 Sq. Ft.

Main	1297 Sq. Ft.
Second	558 Sq. Ft.
Total	1855 Sq. Ft.

ORDER DIRECT
7:00-6:00 Mon.-Fri. CST
800-947-PLAN

VISA   MasterCard   American Express Cards   DISCOVER NOVUS

design basics inc.
HOME PLAN DESIGN SERVICE

GS1330-18 Trenton
PRICE CODE **18**

▶ High quality, erasable, reproducible vellums
▶ Shipped via 2nd day air within the continental U.S.

- entry open to formal dining room with hutch space
- volume great room with see-thru fireplace flooded with natural light from large windows to the back
- hearth kitchen area with bayed dinette, has see-thru fireplace, planning desk and large corner walk-in pantry
- conveniently located powder bath
- main floor mud/laundry area with coat closet and laundry sink
- centralized bathroom convenient for secondary bedrooms
- master suite with sloped ceiling includes walk-in closet, double vanity and corner whirlpool tub

Rear Elevation

Version of GS1380-19 the "Paterson" as seen on page 49.

Parade Home Package
available for all plans

© design basics inc.

Main	1421 Sq. Ft.
Second	448 Sq. Ft.
Total	1869 Sq. Ft.

design basics inc ®
HOME PLAN DESIGN SERVICE

PRICE CODE
GS1867-19 Langley

- ▶ **High quality, erasable, reproducible vellums**
- ▶ **Shipped via 2nd day air within the continental U.S.**

Gold Seal ™
HOME PLANS

- • sleek lines coupled with impressive detailing enhance elevation
- • entry opens into volume great room with fireplace flanked by cheerful windows
- • dining room off great room offers entertaining options

- • kitchen and breakfast area has cooktop in island and access to covered patio
- • bridge overlook on second level
- • secondary bedrooms share compartmented bath with dual lavs

- • master bedroom secluded on first level includes decorative ceiling and bright boxed window
- • luxurious master bath has two closets, separate wet and dry areas, dual lavs and whirlpool tub

Rear Elevation

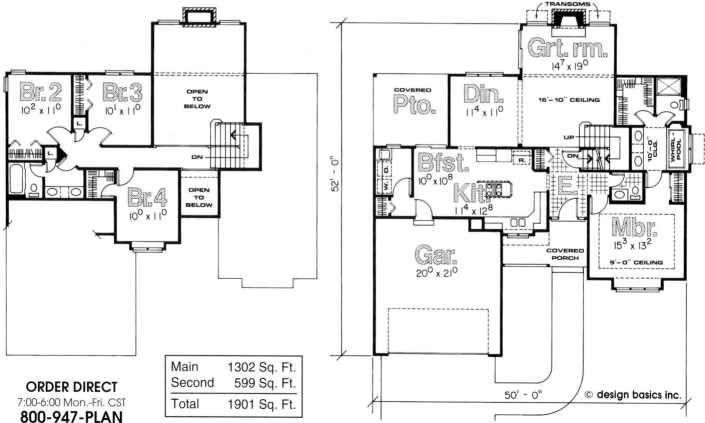

ORDER DIRECT
7:00-6:00 Mon.-Fri. CST
800-947-PLAN

Main	1302 Sq. Ft.	
Second	599 Sq. Ft.	
Total	1901 Sq. Ft.	

© design basics inc.

design basics inc®
HOME PLAN DESIGN SERVICE

GS1727-**19** Spencer

Gold Seal™ HOME PLANS

▸ **High quality, erasable, reproducible vellums**
▸ **Shipped via 2nd day air within the continental U.S.**

- volume hard-surfaced entry with coat closet
- volume ceiling in great room with fireplace flanked by windows
- dining room open to great room for expanded entertaining

- island kitchen adjoins breakfast area with access to covered patio
- laundry room with sink, closet and window to the back
- upstairs landing overlooks entry and great room below

- master bedroom with volume ceiling and arched bayed window adjoins luxury skylit dressing/bath area with whirlpool, walk-in closet and plant shelf
- secondary bedrooms share generous compartmented bath

Rear Elevation

Version of GS1734-17 the "Crescent" as seen on page 57 of Homes of Distinction.

ALL PLANS *Customizable*

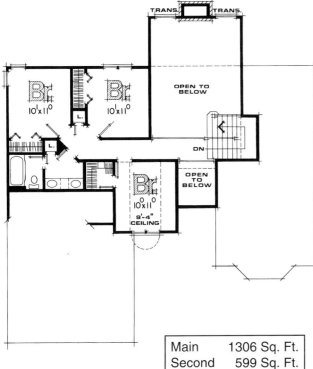

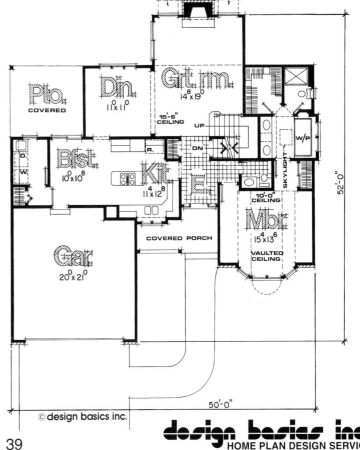

Main	1306 Sq. Ft.
Second	599 Sq. Ft.
Total	1905 Sq. Ft.

ORDER DIRECT
7:00-6:00 Mon.-Fri. CST
800-947-PLAN

© design basics inc.

design basics inc.®
HOME PLAN DESIGN SERVICE

PRICE CODE

GS2551-19 Girard

▸ High quality, erasable, reproducible vellums
▸ Shipped via 2nd day air within the continental U.S.

- convenient for a private home office, French doors off entry reveal an optional den
- staircase to second level is conveniently located at back of house, off of kitchen

- lofty, open great room features raised hearth fireplace flanked by 2 large windows
- wet bar placed for easy access from great room and dinette
- extensive windows and volume ceiling make dinette bright

- seclusion is optimized in well-appointed master suite
- second level front bedroom has delightful window seat and ample walk-in closet

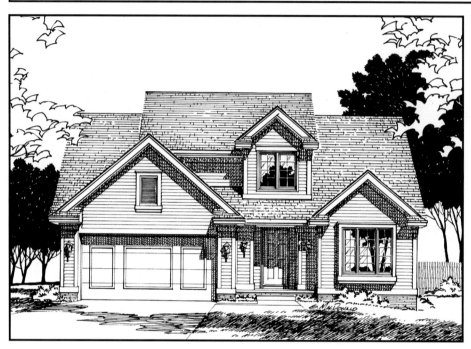

Rear Elevation

Version of GS2486-17 the "Fowler" as seen on page 60 of Homes of Distinction.

Parade Home Package

available for all plans

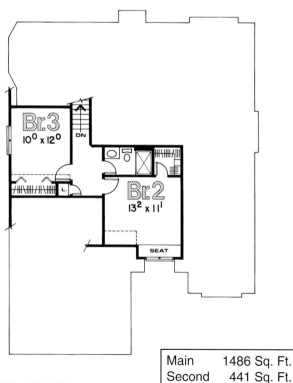

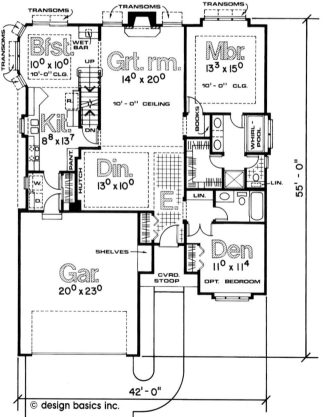

Main	1486 Sq. Ft.
Second	441 Sq. Ft.
Total	1927 Sq. Ft.

© design basics inc.

ORDER DIRECT

7:00-6:00 Mon.-Fri. CST

800-947-PLAN

VISA   MasterCard   WELCOME Cards   DISCOVER NOVUS

design basics inc.®
HOME PLAN DESIGN SERVICE

GS3092-19 Adell

PRICE CODE **19**

Gold Seal HOME PLANS

▶ **High quality, erasable, reproducible vellums**
▶ **Shipped via 2nd day air within the continental U.S.**

- repeating gables create harmonious curb appeal
- unique garage access offers the beauty of a side-load without the expense of an extra-wide lot, plus extra storage

- entry opens to sun-filled great room with 12'-10" ceiling and formal dining room
- dinette has access to rear yard and is open to great room
- kitchen provides large pantry, lazy Susan, snack bar and access to laundry

- French doors open to master suite with well-designed whirlpool bath featuring generous walk-in closet and useful linen closet
- upstairs 3 secondary bedrooms share large bath with built-in linen cabinet

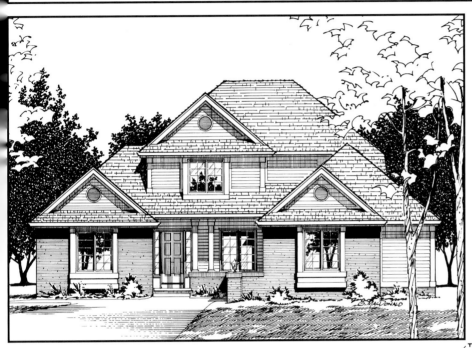

Rear Elevation

Version of GS3089-17 the "Parnell" as seen on page 56 of Homes of Distinction.

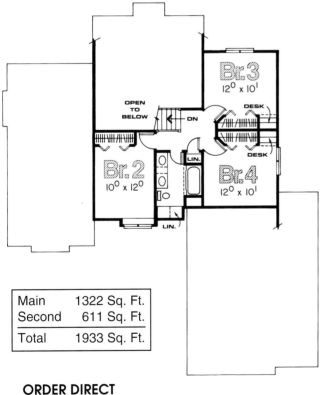

Main	1322 Sq. Ft.
Second	611 Sq. Ft.
Total	1933 Sq. Ft.

ORDER DIRECT
7:00-6:00 Mon.-Fri. CST
800-947-PLAN

design basics inc.®
HOME PLAN DESIGN SERVICE

© design basics inc.

PRICE CODE

GS2292-**19** Inglewood

▶ **High quality, erasable, reproducible vellums**
▶ **Shipped via 2nd day air within the continental U.S.**

- stone accents and inviting porch enrich front elevation
- entry views volume great room with captivating window-framed fireplace
- formal dining area allows entertaining ease

- gourmet island kitchen has snack bar, handy desk and walk-in pantry
- dinette has access to large covered patio ideal for leisure activities
- two secondary bedrooms share a roomy bath with its own linen closet

- handy unfinished storage on second level
- French doors open to pampering main level master suite with boxed ceiling
- master dressing area with two closets, dual lavs with knee space between and window-brightened whirlpool

Rear Elevation

Version of GS2220-21 the "Gentry" as seen on page 63.

ALL PLANS *Customizable*

Main	1507 Sq. Ft.
Second	436 Sq. Ft.
Total	1943 Sq. Ft.

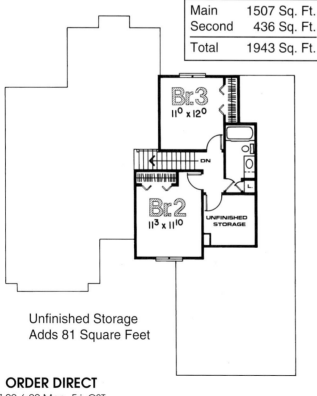

Unfinished Storage
Adds 81 Square Feet

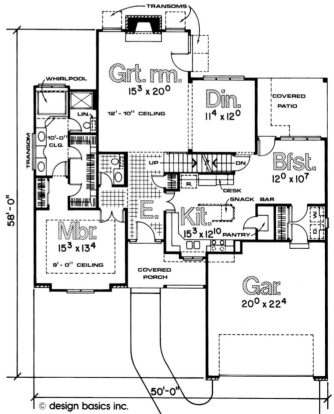

© design basics inc.

design basics inc.
HOME PLAN DESIGN SERVICE

GS2554-19 Lansing
PRICE CODE

▶ High quality, erasable, reproducible vellums
▶ Shipped via 2nd day air within the continental U.S.

- rhythmic use of arches creates a notable elevation
- practical use of space is demonstrated by the placement of 2 closets in the entry
- optional den is accentuated by dramatic windows and a dramatic ceiling

- lofty open great room features a fireplace flanked by large windows
- dinette featuring a desk and snack bar also provides convenient access to the outdoors
- garage features built-in workbench

- master suite features a deluxe bath with whirlpool and dual lavs and large walk-in closet
- second level front bedroom achieves a feeling of spaciousness with a 10-foot ceiling and arch-top window

Rear Elevation

Version of GS2330-17 the "Pomeroy" as seen on page 58 of Homes of Distinction.

PARADE Home Package
available for all plans

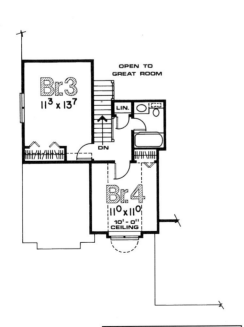

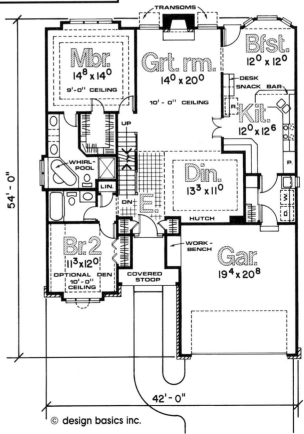

© design basics inc.

ORDER DIRECT
7:00-6:00 Mon.-Fri. CST
800-947-PLAN

VISA MasterCard American Express Cards DISCOVER NOVUS

Main	1517 Sq. Ft.
Second	431 Sq. Ft.
Total	1948 Sq. Ft.

design basics inc®
HOME PLAN DESIGN SERVICE

PRICE CODE

GS2219-19 Shannon

▶ High quality, erasable, reproducible vellums
▶ Shipped via 2nd day air within the continental U.S.

Gold Seal
HOME PLANS ™

- quaint covered porch
- formal dining room with elegant bayed window seen from entry
- large windows flank handsome fireplace in great room
- beautiful bayed dinette

- snack bar, pantry and window above the sink in kitchen
- convenient main floor laundry room
- extra storage in garage
- tiered ceiling and corner windows in master bedroom

- pampering master dressing/bath area features two closets, double vanity and angled whirlpool in corner under window
- 3 bedrooms on second level served by hall bath

Rear Elevation

Version of GS2281-17 the "Ingram" as seen on page 61 of Homes of Distinction.

PROMOTIONAL LICENSE
Black and White, Camera-Ready Artwork of the home plan FREE with any plan purchase to assist you in advertising the home.

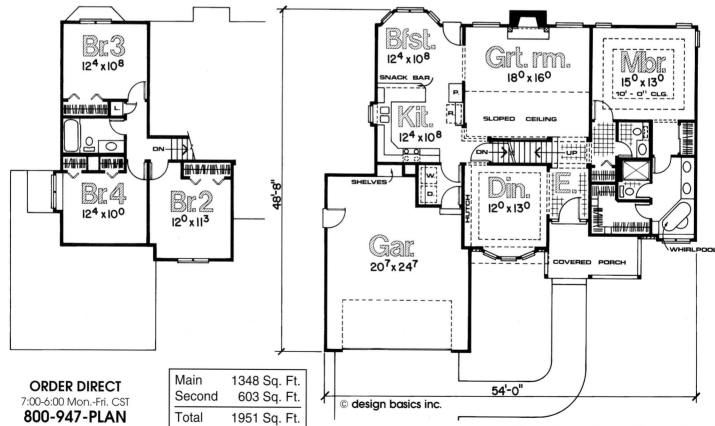

ORDER DIRECT
7:00-6:00 Mon.-Fri. CST
800-947-PLAN

VISA MasterCard AMERICAN EXPRESS Cards DISCOVER NOVUS

Main	1348	Sq. Ft.
Second	603	Sq. Ft.
Total	1951	Sq. Ft.

© design basics inc.

design basics inc.®
HOME PLAN DESIGN SERVICE

44

PRICE CODE
GS3063-19 Taylor

▶ High quality, erasable, reproducible vellums
▶ Shipped via 2nd day air within the continental U.S.

- country style elevation highlighted by detailed porch and brick accents
- formal dining room proudly welcomes guests at entry

- well-integrated family room, kitchen and breakfast area accommodate many family activities
- master suite contains 10-foot-high ceilings while angled doors in the whirlpool bath add drama

- 3 secondary bedrooms share roomy hall bath serviced by large linen
- ample unfinished storage is a great feature in this 1½ story home

Rear Elevation

Version of GS3076-17 the "Sayler" as seen on page 64 of Homes Of Distinction.

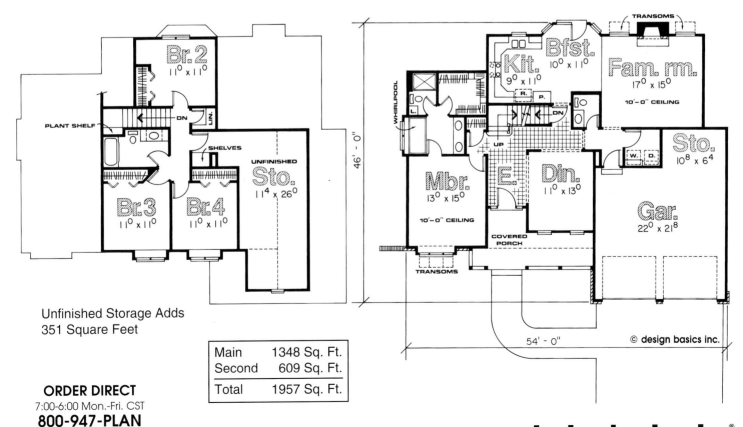

Unfinished Storage Adds 351 Square Feet

Main	1348 Sq. Ft.
Second	609 Sq. Ft.
Total	1957 Sq. Ft.

ORDER DIRECT
7:00-6:00 Mon.-Fri. CST
800-947-PLAN

design basics inc.®
HOME PLAN DESIGN SERVICE

GS2719-19 Eldorado

PRICE CODE

▶ High quality, erasable, reproducible vellums
▶ Shipped via 2nd day air within the continental U.S.

- angled porch, with wood railing, and shutter treatments inspire country mood
- majestic great room beckons with high ceiling and sunny, tall windows framing fireplace

- well-designed kitchen offers daily cooking ease while bright dinette has exit to outdoors
- spacious master bath features angled whirlpool, dual lavs, shower and spacious walk-in closet

- three bedrooms and bath complete livable upper level
- large storage space in garage area helps maximize full usage of home

Rear Elevation

Parade Home Package

available for all plans

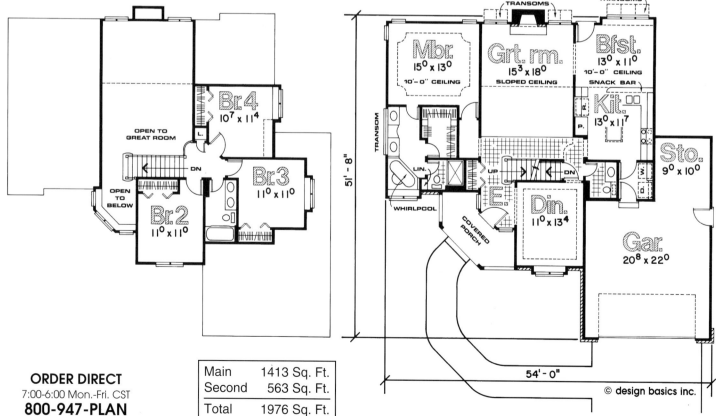

ORDER DIRECT

7:00-6:00 Mon.-Fri. CST

800-947-PLAN

Main	1413 Sq. Ft.
Second	563 Sq. Ft.
Total	1976 Sq. Ft.

© design basics inc.

design basics inc.
HOME PLAN DESIGN SERVICE

46

GS3556-**19** Pottersville

PRICE CODE

- comfortable elevation reveals its family style
- wrapping front porch
- oak entry showcases U-shaped staircase
- dining room expands entry and has intricate ceiling detail

- French doors lead to island kitchen flooded with light from bayed breakfast area
- family room with cathedral ceiling and fireplace also benefits from snack bar

- master bedroom has volume ceiling and romantic bath with whirlpool
- laundry room offers soaking sink
- large garage with handy storage closet

Rear Elevation

Version of GS3557-17 the "Edison" as seen on page 65 of Homes of Distinction.

PROMOTIONAL LICENSE • Black and White, Camera-Ready Artwork of the home plan FREE with any plan purchase to assist you in advertising the home.

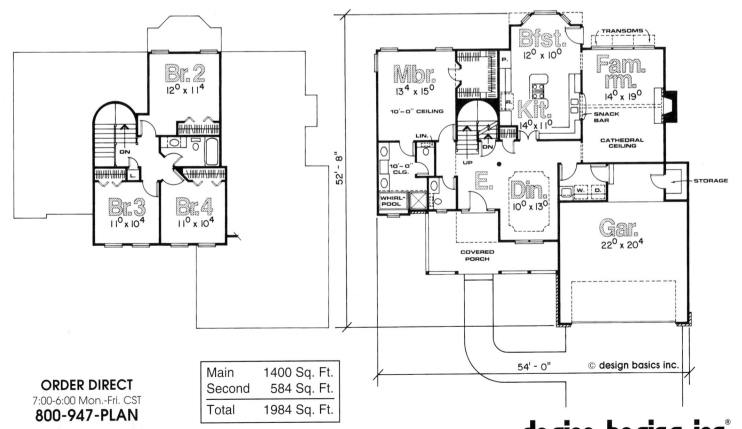

Main	1400 Sq. Ft.
Second	584 Sq. Ft.
Total	1984 Sq. Ft.

design basics inc.®
HOME PLAN DESIGN SERVICE

PRICE CODE
GS3382-19 Higgins

▶ High quality, erasable, reproducible vellums
▶ Shipped via 2nd day air within the continental U.S.

- notable exterior features captivate attention
- bayed windows and vaulted ceiling displayed in dining room
- snack bar and boxed window above sink accommodate kitchen

- breakfast area enhanced by two corner boxed windows
- great room unfolds tall windows framing fireplace
- secluded master suite reveals roomy walk-in closet and sunny whirlpool

- bedroom #3 has 10'-0" ceiling and bayed window with arched transom
- all three secondary bedrooms are served by full bath

Rear Elevation

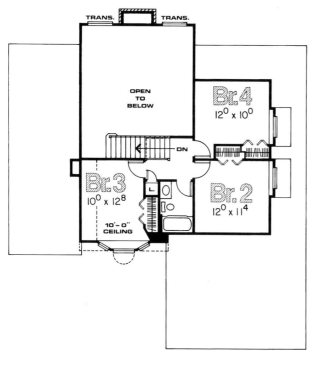

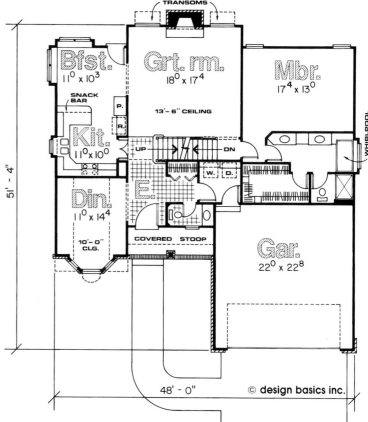

ORDER DIRECT
7:00-6:00 Mon.-Fri. CST
800-947-PLAN

Main	1424 Sq. Ft.
Second	567 Sq. Ft.
Total	1991 Sq. Ft.

VISA MasterCard AMERICAN EXPRESS Cards DISCOVER NOVUS

© design basics inc.

design basics inc.
HOME PLAN DESIGN SERVICE

GS1380-19 Paterson

PRICE CODE

Gold Seal ™
HOME PLANS

- inviting front porch welcomes guests
- hard-surfaced entryway is open to formal dining room with hutch space
- volume great room with generous windows and cozy, see-thru fireplace is open to entry

- hearth kitchen with bayed breakfast area and large planning desk
- main floor laundry area with coat closet and laundry sink doubles as mud entry from garage

- elegant sloped ceiling in master suite with pampering bath which includes double vanity, walk-in closet and window above the whirlpool tub
- future expansion possible over garage with access off hall

Rear Elevation

Version of GS1330-18 the "Trenton" as seen on page 37.

PARADE Home Package
available for all plans

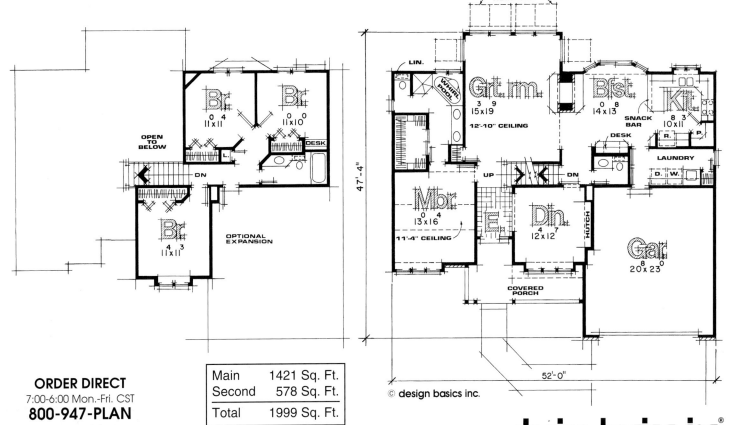

© design basics inc.

Main	1421 Sq. Ft.
Second	578 Sq. Ft.
Total	1999 Sq. Ft.

design basics inc.®
HOME PLAN DESIGN SERVICE

49

GS1863-19 Andover

PRICE CODE

Gold Seal HOME PLANS™

▶ High quality, erasable, reproducible vellums
▶ Shipped via 2nd day air within the continental U.S.

- covered porch and lovely details lend peaceful flavor to elevation
- volume entry hall with view of formal dining room and luxurious great room
- volume ceiling and abundant windows highlight great room

- kitchen/breakfast area features see-thru fireplace, snack bar, desk, walk-in pantry and wrapping counters
- windowed laundry room has soaking sink
- bedroom #3 has arched window, bedroom #4 has built-in desk

- master suite secluded on main level features vaulted ceiling
- luxurious bath/dressing area includes roomy walk-in closet, dual lavs and corner whirlpool tub

Rear Elevation

PROMOTIONAL LICENSE • PROMOTIONAL LICENSE • PROMOTIONAL LICENSE • PROMOTIONAL LICENSE

Black and White, Camera-Ready Artwork of the home plan FREE with any plan purchase to assist you in advertising the home.

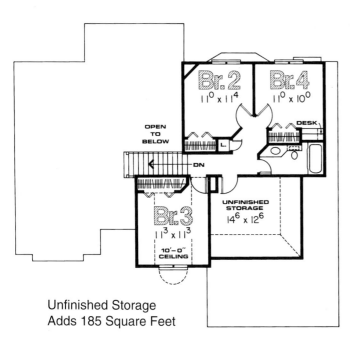

Unfinished Storage
Adds 185 Square Feet

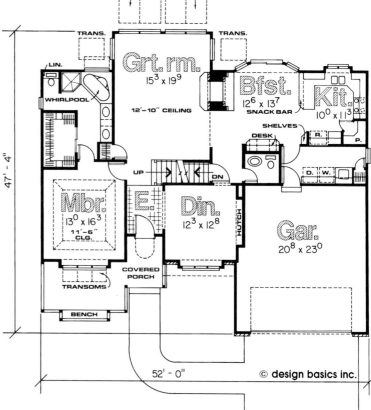

ORDER DIRECT
7:00-6:00 Mon.-Fri. CST
800-947-PLAN

VISA MasterCard American Express Cards Discover NOVUS

Main	1421 Sq. Ft.
Second	578 Sq. Ft.
Total	1999 Sq. Ft.

© design basics inc.

design basics inc.®
HOME PLAN DESIGN SERVICE

Gold Seal™
HOME PLANS

▶ High quality, erasable, reproducible vellums
▶ Shipped via 2nd day air within the continental U.S.

- volume entry with view to great room
- sloped ceiling to nearly 17-foot-high in great room with bright windows and impressive fireplace
- large dining room with hutch space
- extra storage in garage

- efficient island kitchen with pantries and planning desk
- sunny dinette with large plant window ledges
- private master suite with interesting ceiling detail

- deluxe dressing/bath area with his and her vanities, 2-person whirlpool tub and walk-in closet
- upstairs landing overlooks great room and entry
- walk-in closet in bedroom #2

Rear Elevation

Version of GS1018-21 the "Maximum" as seen on page 67.

ALL PLANS *Customizable*

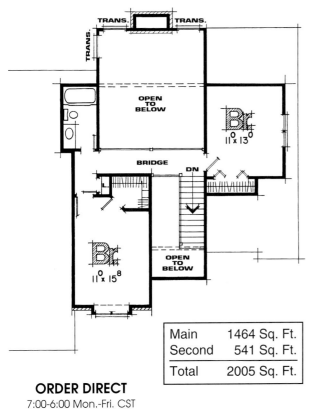

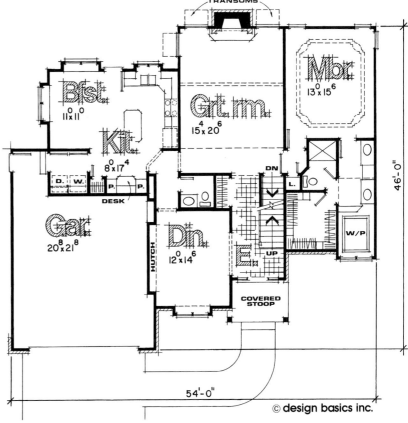

Main	1464 Sq. Ft.
Second	541 Sq. Ft.
Total	2005 Sq. Ft.

ORDER DIRECT
7:00-6:00 Mon.-Fri. CST
800-947-PLAN

VISA   MasterCard   AMERICAN EXPRESS Cards   DISCOVER NOVUS

© design basics inc.

design basics inc.®
HOME PLAN DESIGN SERVICE

GS3075-20 Grant

PRICE CODE

Gold Seal™ HOME PLANS

▶ **High quality, erasable, reproducible vellums**
▶ **Shipped via 2nd day air within the continental U.S.**

- gabled roof and limited brick use add affordability to this great elevation
- elegant U-stairs, French doors to kitchen and views to formal dining and great rooms create wonderful entry

- great room has cathedral ceiling, brick fireplace between large windows and direct access to breakfast area
- efficient kitchen offers corner sink, 2 pantries, lazy Susan and snack bar

- large laundry with sink and closet
- master suite has atrium door to rear yard, great whirlpool bath with open shower and generous walk-in closet
- upstairs, 3 secondary bedrooms share compartmented bath

Rear Elevation

Version of GS3065-18 the "Foster" as seen on page 34.

Parade Home Package
available for all plans

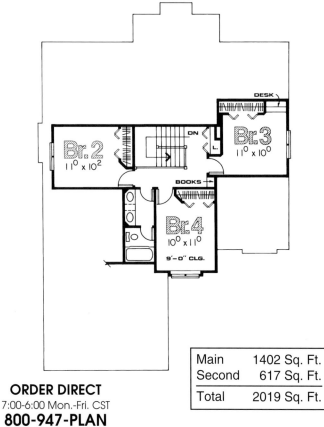

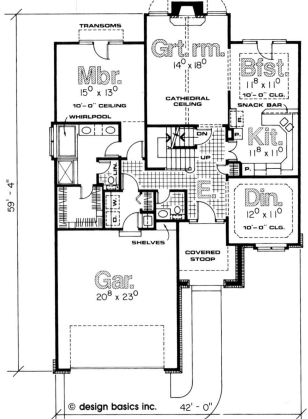

Main	1402 Sq. Ft.
Second	617 Sq. Ft.
Total	2019 Sq. Ft.

ORDER DIRECT
7:00-6:00 Mon.-Fri. CST
800-947-PLAN

design basics inc®
HOME PLAN DESIGN SERVICE

PRICE CODE

GS3381-20 Amanda

Gold Seal™ HOME PLANS

- ▶ High quality, erasable, reproducible vellums
- ▶ Shipped via 2nd day air within the continental U.S.

- traditional features enhance cozy appeal
- dining room with dropped perimeter ceiling and bayed windows offers perfect view of refinement
- picture awning windows frame fireplace in great room with 2-story high sloped ceiling
- bayed breakfast area gives view and access to backyard
- kitchen designed to be easily accessible to and from breakfast area, dining room and garage
- secluded master suite provides tiered 10-foot ceiling, corner whirlpool and spacious walk-in closet
- second floor bath serves three roomy bedrooms
- plant shelf garnishes the entry

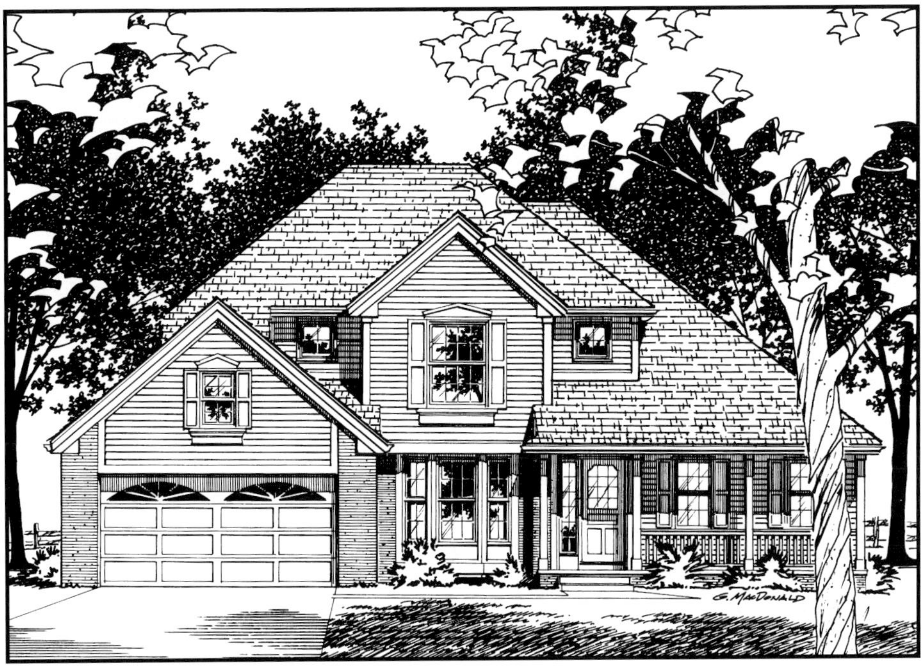
G. MacDONALD

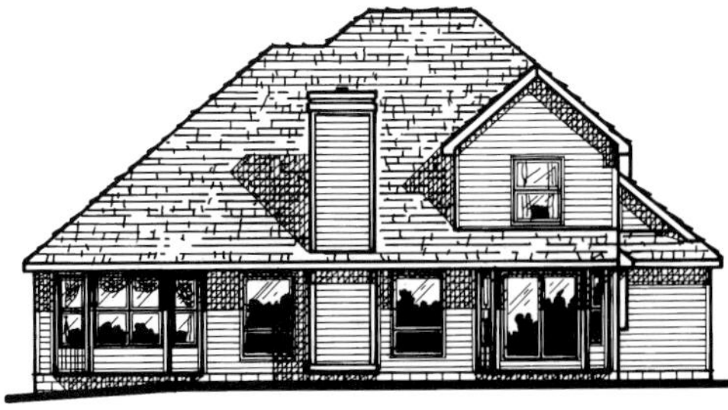

Rear Elevation

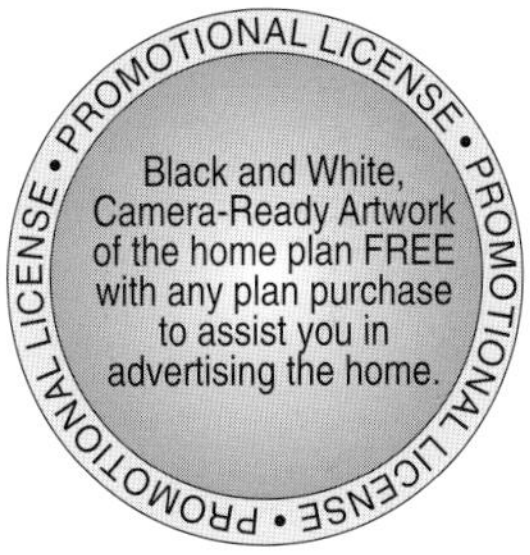
PROMOTIONAL LICENSE • PROMOTIONAL LICENSE • PROMOTIONAL LICENSE •
Black and White, Camera-Ready Artwork of the home plan FREE with any plan purchase to assist you in advertising the home.

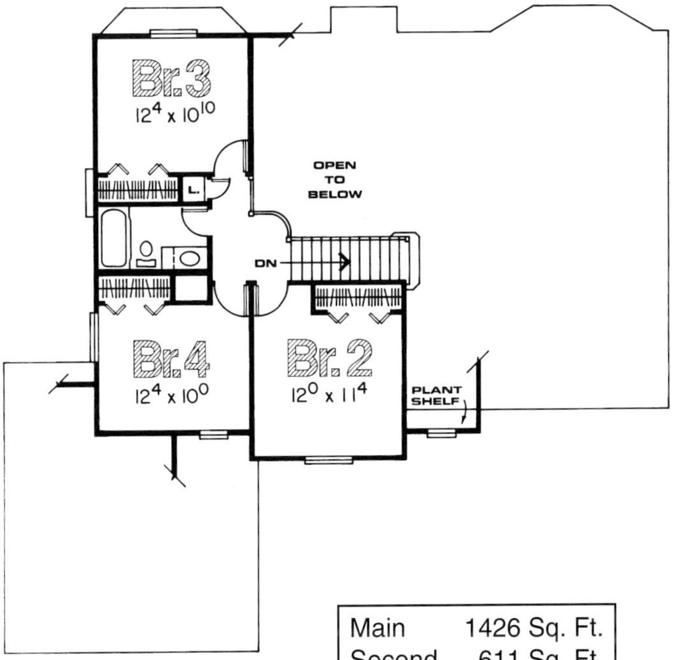
Br.3
12⁴ x 10¹⁰
L.
OPEN TO BELOW
DN
Br.4
12⁴ x 10⁰
Br.2
12⁰ x 11⁴
PLANT SHELF

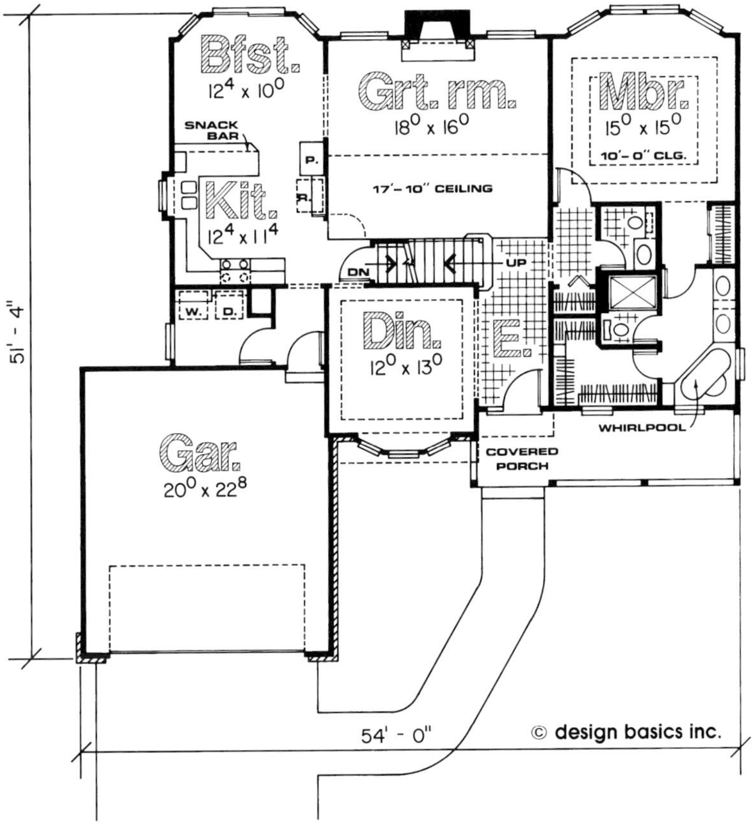
Bfst.
12⁴ x 10⁰
SNACK BAR
Kit.
12⁴ x 11⁴
P.
R.
Grt. rm.
18⁰ x 16⁰
17'-10" CEILING
Mbr.
15⁰ x 15⁰
10'-0" CLG.
DN
UP
W.
D.
Din.
12⁰ x 13⁰
E.
WHIRLPOOL
COVERED PORCH
Gar.
20⁰ x 22⁸
51' - 4"
54' - 0"

© design basics inc.

Main	1426 Sq. Ft.
Second	611 Sq. Ft.
Total	2037 Sq. Ft.

ORDER DIRECT
7:00-6:00 Mon.-Fri. CST
800-947-PLAN
VISA MasterCard American Express Cards Discover Novus

design basics inc.®
HOME PLAN DESIGN SERVICE

PRICE CODE

GS3064-20 Eldridge

▶ High quality, erasable, reproducible vellums
▶ Shipped via 2nd day air within the continental U.S.

Gold Seal HOME PLANS

- covered porch, bayed window and column details accent this 1½ story home
- entry reveals formal dining room and spacious great room with fireplace and 10-foot-high ceiling
- octagon-shaped breakfast area is enhanced by arched transom windows
- roomy island kitchen features snack bar, lazy Susan and pantry
- master suite offers large walk-in closet, dual lavs, whirlpool bath and shower area
- efficient laundry has convenient access from garage and kitchen
- dual linen closets serve upstairs hall bath with dual lavs

Rear Elevation

ALL PLANS *Customizable*

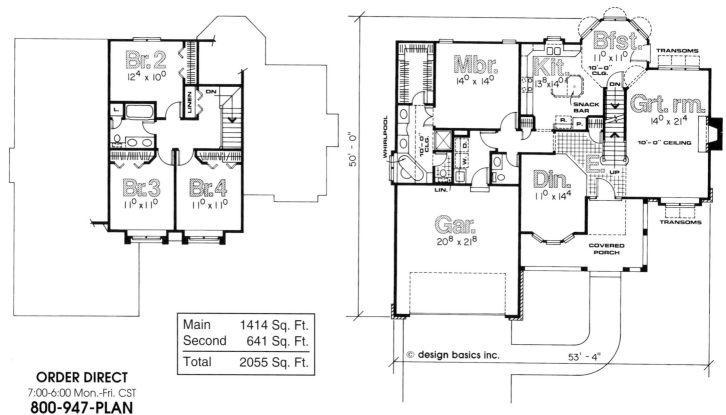

Main	1414 Sq. Ft.
Second	641 Sq. Ft.
Total	2055 Sq. Ft.

ORDER DIRECT
7:00-6:00 Mon.-Fri. CST
800-947-PLAN

54

design basics inc.
HOME PLAN DESIGN SERVICE

PRICE CODE
GS1057-20 Brockton

▶ **High quality, erasable, reproducible vellums**
▶ **Shipped via 2nd day air within the continental U.S.**

Gold Seal
HOME PLANS

- formal dining room defined with columns open to entry
- dramatic open staircase
- efficient kitchen with pantry, corner range and wet bar/salad sink
- mud room/laundry at garage entry

- beautiful dinette with gazebo feeling
- volume ceiling in great room with fireplace framed by windows
- master bedroom with deluxe bath area including double vanity, corner shower and whirlpool tub

- core hallway to secondary bedrooms
- one secondary bedroom features walk-in closet
- centralized clothes chute and linen closet for upstairs bedrooms

Rear Elevation

ALL DESIGN BASICS PLANS HAVE BEEN REGISTERED
ORIGINAL © DRAFT
WITH THE U.S. COPYRIGHT OFFICE

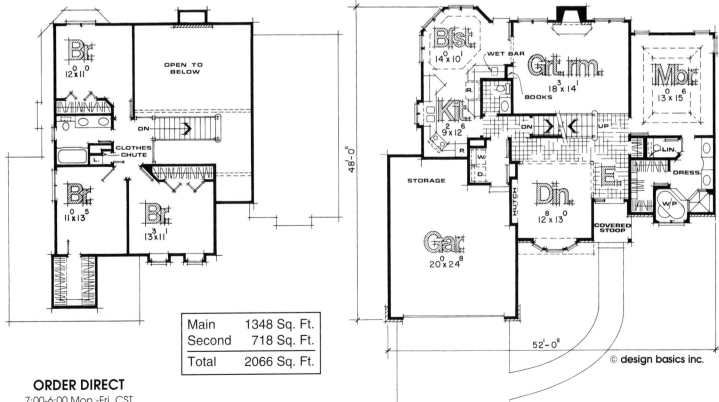

Main	1348 Sq. Ft.
Second	718 Sq. Ft.
Total	**2066 Sq. Ft.**

© design basics inc.

ORDER DIRECT
7:00-6:00 Mon.-Fri. CST
800-947-PLAN

design basics inc.®
HOME PLAN DESIGN SERVICE

GS3537-20 Samuels

PRICE CODE **20**

- ▶ High quality, erasable, reproducible vellums
- ▶ Shipped via 2nd day air within the continental U.S.

- candid country atmosphere is created by a bright elevation
- formal dining room extends feeling of spaciousness from roomy entry hall
- kitchen/breakfast area has bayed windows, snack bar and two lazy Susans
- 10'-7" ceiling and fireplace in family room
- master bedroom enriched with bayed windows and 10'-0" high ceiling
- dual sink vanity, whirlpool, open shower and massive walk-in closet in master bath
- secondary bedrooms graced with arched windows and 10'-0" ceiling
- second floor balcony with view of entry
- mud entry offers nice pathway from garage

Rear Elevation

Version on GS3536-17 the "Clemens" as seen on page 59 of Homes of Distinction.

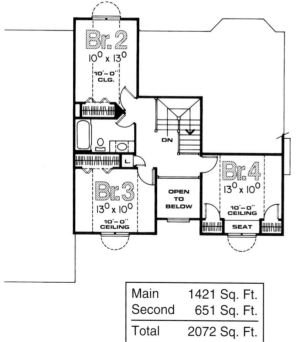

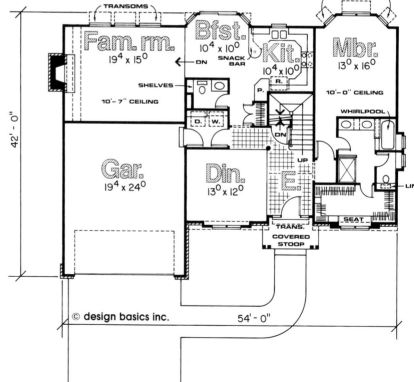

Main	1421 Sq. Ft.
Second	651 Sq. Ft.
Total	2072 Sq. Ft.

ORDER DIRECT
7:00-6:00 Mon.-Fri. CST
800-947-PLAN

GS2745-20 Sierra

PRICE CODE

▶ High quality, erasable, reproducible vellums
▶ Shipped via 2nd day air within the continental U.S.

- unique angled front elevation with covered porch gives this plan distinctive personality
- 2nd story ceiling of the entry continues into the massive great room
- 3-sided fireplace opens to great room, kitchen and dinette
- convenient main level laundry is made even more practical with both kitchen and garage access
- master bedroom is detailed with built-in dresser, spacious bath and walk-in closet
- secondary bedrooms are serviced by large bath with dual lavs

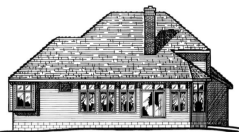

Rear Elevation

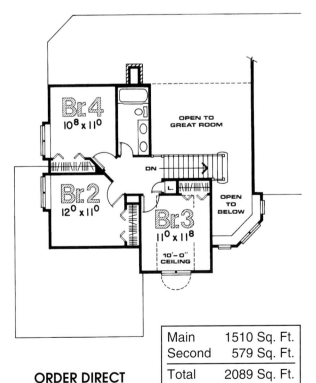

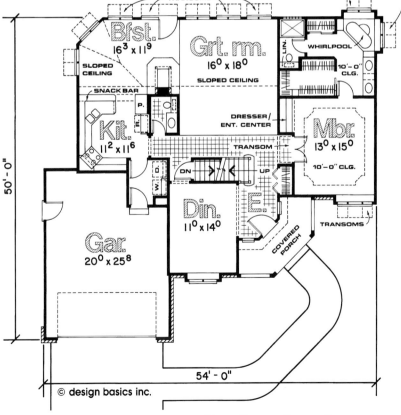

Main	1510 Sq. Ft.
Second	579 Sq. Ft.
Total	2089 Sq. Ft.

© design basics inc.

ORDER DIRECT
7:00-6:00 Mon.-Fri. CST
800-947-PLAN

design basics inc.
HOME PLAN DESIGN SERVICE

BUY HERE. CHANGE HERE.

WHY?

CONVENIENCE

All of the time-saving, hassle-free benefits of one-stop shopping are yours when you allow us to make changes to your Design Basics plan.

PLAN FAMILIARITY

Because our in-house designers are intimately familiar with each plan, you can be assured design integrity will be maintained, regardless of the change.

ACCURACY

Our highly-detailed, multiple review process ensures accurate execution of each Design Basics plan change.

STRUCTURAL ENGINEERING

As a point of reference, each plan change is structurally engineered in accordance with standard codes for Design Basics' local area (Omaha, NE).

ALL PLANS *Customizable*

DESIGN BASICS PLAN CHANGE

······ DIRECTORY ······
OF MOST COMMONLY REQUESTED CHANGES

CALL US TOLL-FREE AT
(800) 947-7526

As a part of our commitment to help you achieve the "perfect" home, we offer an extensive variety of plan changes for any Design Basics plan. For those whose decision to purchase a home plan is contingent upon the feasibility of a plan change, our Customer Support Specialists will, in most cases, be able to provide a FREE price quote for the changes.

CUSTOM CHANGES  PRICES

2 X 6 EXTERIOR WALLS .... $150 ....
FROM STANDARD 2 X 4 TO 2 X 6 EXTERIOR WALLS

EACH GARAGE ALTERATION .... $275 ....

- •FRONT-ENTRY TO SIDE LOAD (OR VICE VERSA)
- •2-CAR TO 3-CAR (OR VICE VERSA)
- •2-CAR FRONT-ENTRY TO 3-CAR SIDE-LOAD (OR VICE VERSA)
- •3-CAR FRONT-ENTRY TO 2-CAR SIDE-LOAD (OR VICE VERSA)

WALK-OUT BASEMENT .... $175 ....

CRAWL SPACE FOUNDATION .... $225 ....

SLAB FOUNDATION .... $225 ....

STRETCH CHANGES (SEE EXAMPLE NEXT PAGE) .... $5 per lineal foot of cut

ADDITIONAL BRICK TO SIDES & REAR .... $325 ....

ADDITIONAL BRICK TO FRONT,
    SIDES AND REAR .... $425 ....

ALTERNATE PRELIMINARY ELEVATION .... $150 ....

9 FOOT MAIN LEVEL WALLS .... starting at $150

SPECIFY WINDOW BRAND .... $95 ....

POURED CONCRETE FOUNDATION .... $25 ....
ONLY WITH OTHER CHANGES

ADDING ONE COURSE (8") TO THE
    FOUNDATION HEIGHT .... $25 ....
ONLY WITH OTHER CHANGES

NOTE _____

- • All plan changes come to you on erasable reproducible vellums.
- • An unchanged set of original vellums is available for only $50 along with your plan changes.
- • Gold Seal™ changes are not made to the artist's renderings, electrical, sections or cabinets.
- • Prices are subject to change.

Call us toll-free at (800) 947-7526 to answer questions you may have or to schedule any changes not found in this directory.

A CUSTOM CHANGE SOLUTION
STRETCH CHANGES

PROBLEM:

A. & B.) Secondary bedrooms seemed too tight for owner's existing furniture.

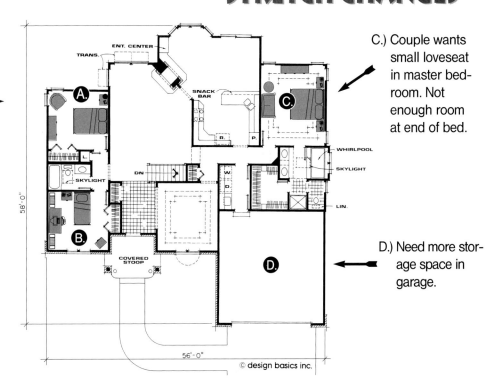

C.) Couple wants small loveseat in master bedroom. Not enough room at end of bed.

D.) Need more storage space in garage.

SOLUTION:

A.) A 2' stretch to the left side of the home allows for a 3' walkway between the chair and end of bed. Three feet is a comfortable distance for passage.

B.) That 2' stretch loosens up the traffic flow and adds extra room to move around the desk area.

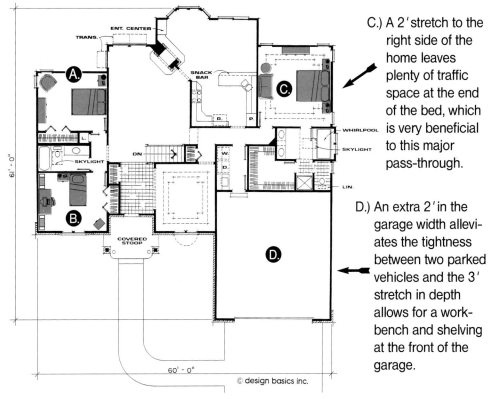

C.) A 2' stretch to the right side of the home leaves plenty of traffic space at the end of the bed, which is very beneficial to this major pass-through.

D.) An extra 2' in the garage width alleviates the tightness between two parked vehicles and the 3' stretch in depth allows for a workbench and shelving at the front of the garage.

Sometimes it is easier to understand the need for custom changes by envisioning the home furnished. As illustrated above, Design Basics Study Print and Furniture Layout Guide provides a 1/4"- scale floor plan and re-usable 1/4"- scale furniture pieces to help you imagine how a specific home will live. For more information, see the back page of this publication.

GS2951-21 Newlin
PRICE CODE 21

► High quality, erasable, reproducible vellums
► Shipped via 2nd day air within the continental U.S.

- brick wing walls anchor magnificent elevation
- formal dining room is enriched by 2-story entry
- great room enhanced by 10-foot-high ceiling and brick fireplace

- exciting kitchen provides corner sink, large pantry and snack bar
- spacious dinette with large windows has access to back yard

- master suite features whirlpool bath, open shower and ceiling detail
- second level bridge overlooks entry and staircase
- secondary bedrooms share large bath and deep linen closet

Rear Elevation

Parade Home Package
available for all plans

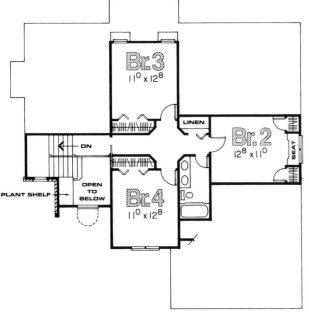

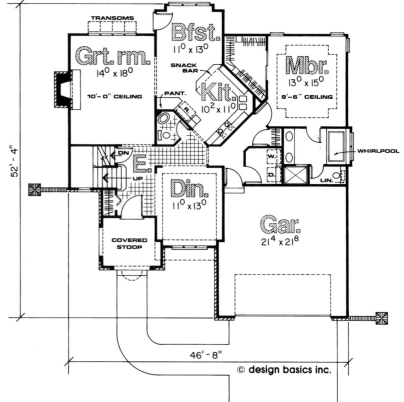

© design basics inc.

ORDER DIRECT
7:00-6:00 Mon.-Fri. CST
800-947-PLAN

Main	1406	Sq. Ft.
Second	703	Sq. Ft.
Total	2109	Sq. Ft.

design basics inc.
HOME PLAN DESIGN SERVICE

PRICE CODE

GS2312-21 Meredith

▶ High quality, erasable, reproducible vellums
▶ Shipped via 2nd day air within the continental U.S.

- volume entry surveys formal living and dining rooms
- window-brightened living and dining rooms ideal for entertaining
- cheery fireplace and sloped ceiling in family room

- amenable kitchen/dinette with snack bar, two lazy Susans and ample counters enjoys easy access to family room
- loft or optional bedroom #4 open to below is ideal for a study/game room

- secondary bedrooms enjoy ample bath and huge walk-in linen closet
- exquisite master suite secluded on first floor includes pampering master dressing/bath with huge walk-in closet, his and her lavs and whirlpool

Rear Elevation

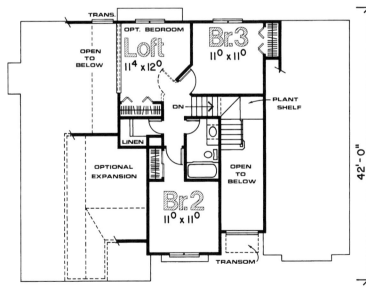

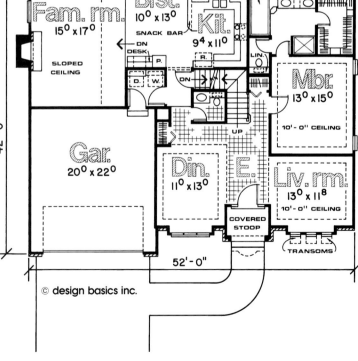

© design basics inc.

Optional Expansion Adds
246 Square Feet

Main	1519 Sq. Ft.
Second	594 Sq. Ft.
Total	2113 Sq. Ft.

ORDER DIRECT
7:00-6:00 Mon.-Fri. CST
800-947-PLAN

design basics inc.®
HOME PLAN DESIGN SERVICE

GS2285-21 Prairie

Gold Seal
HOME PLANS ™

▶ High quality, erasable, reproducible vellums
▶ Shipped via 2nd day air within the continental U.S.

- expansive front elevation enhanced by covered porch alludes to sophisticated interior
- dramatic entry surveys dining room with hutch space and elegant great room beyond
- expansiveness of great room is enriched by cathedral ceiling and trapezoid windows
- kitchen/breakfast area with nearby laundry and powder bath is designed for convenience and ease of living
- secondary bedrooms secluded on second level, bedroom #4 with volume ceiling and arched window
- main floor master suite contains skylit dressing area, corner whirlpool and spacious walk-in closet

Rear Elevation

ORIGINAL DRAFT
ALL DESIGN BASICS PLANS HAVE BEEN REGISTERED
WITH THE U.S. COPYRIGHT OFFICE.
©

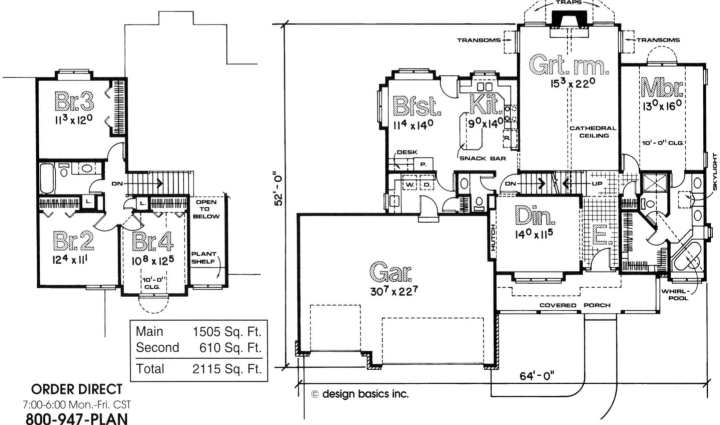

Main	1505 SQ. FT.
Second	610 SQ. FT.
Total	2115 SQ. FT.

© design basics inc.

ORDER DIRECT
7:00–6:00 Mon.-Fri. CST
800-947-PLAN

VISA   MasterCard   AMERICAN EXPRESS Cards   DISCOVER NOVUS

design basics inc. ®
HOME PLAN DESIGN SERVICE

GS2220-21 Gentry

PRICE CODE

► High quality, erasable, reproducible vellums
► Shipped via 2nd day air within the continental U.S.

- arched window is seen in volume entry
- volume great room with handsome fireplace and windows out the back
- service doors to close off kitchen
- dining room and dinette both feature large windows out the back

- gourmet kitchen includes snack bar on island counter, desk and walk-in pantry
- convenient family entrance through laundry with closet
- beautiful arched window, double doors and sloped ceiling in master suite

- master dressing area includes 2-person whirlpool, his and her vanities and decorator plant ledge
- compartmented hall bath serves secondary bedrooms

Rear Elevation

Version of GS2292-19 the "Inglewood" as seen on page 42.

Parade Home Package
available for all plans

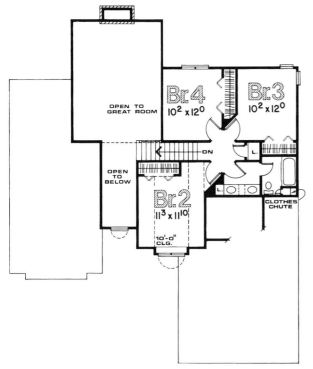

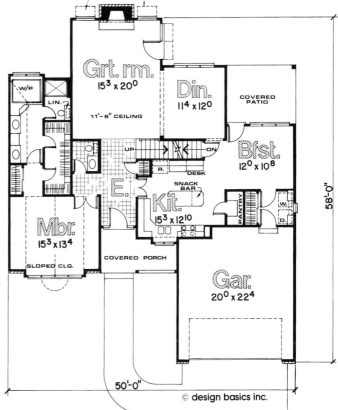

© design basics inc.

ORDER DIRECT
7:00-6:00 Mon.-Fri. CST
800-947-PLAN

VISA MasterCard AMERICAN EXPRESS Cards DISCOVER NOVUS

Main	1506 Sq. Ft.
Second	633 Sq. Ft.
Total	2139 Sq. Ft.

design basics inc.®
HOME PLAN DESIGN SERVICE

PRICE CODE

GS1417-21 Sanborn

Gold Seal
HOME PLANS™

▶ **High quality, erasable, reproducible vellums**
▶ **Shipped via 2nd day air within the continental U.S.**

- diagonal views through house from entry
- 10-foot ceilings at entry and in living and dining areas
- volume living room with sunny bayed window and handsome fireplace

- formal dining room with hutch space
- service entry from garage through laundry/mud room with coat closet
- French doors into deluxe master bedroom

- skylit master bath/dressing area with whirlpool and large walk-in closet
- upstairs corridor hall connects secondary bedrooms
- large linen closet in compartmented bath with double lavs

Rear Elevation

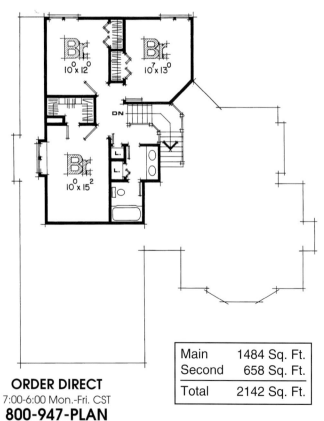

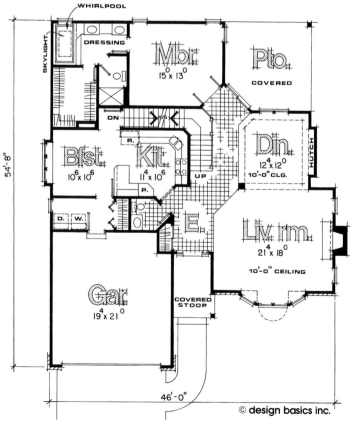

Main	1484 Sq. Ft.
Second	658 Sq. Ft.
Total	2142 Sq. Ft.

ORDER DIRECT

7:00-6:00 Mon.-Fri. CST

800-947-PLAN

© design basics inc.

design basics inc.®
HOME PLAN DESIGN SERVICE

GS2328-21 Birchley

PRICE CODE

▶ High quality, erasable, reproducible vellums
▶ Shipped via 2nd day air within the continental U.S.

- alluring brick elevation
- entry includes roomy closet
- openness of dining room enhanced by elegant columns
- great room with bright windows includes raised hearth fireplace

- kitchen and bayed breakfast area support leisure or entertaining activities
- second floor features optional den/loft with built-in desk and bookshelves
- bath with dual lavs serves secondary bedrooms

- elegant main floor master bedroom enjoys privacy, special window and tiered ceiling
- pampering bath/dressing area features whirlpool, his and her vanities and large walk-in closet

Rear Elevation

Main	1509 Sq. Ft.
Second	661 Sq. Ft.
Total	2170 Sq. Ft.

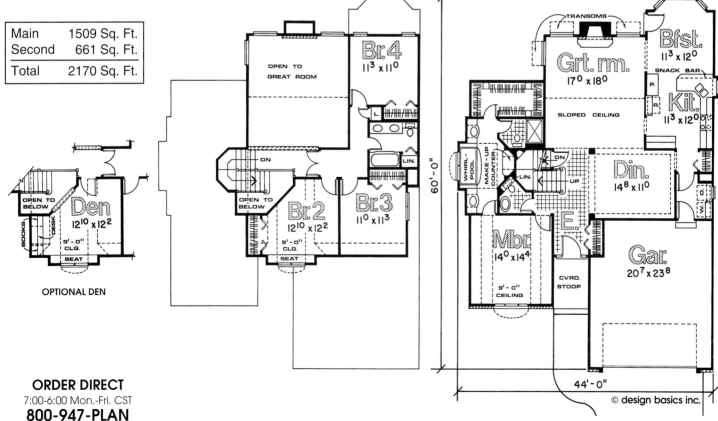

OPTIONAL DEN

ORDER DIRECT
7:00-6:00 Mon.-Fri. CST
800-947-PLAN

© design basics inc.

design basics inc.®
HOME PLAN DESIGN SERVICE

PRICE CODE

GS3081-21 Gladstone

- ▶ High quality, erasable, reproducible vellums
- ▶ Shipped via 2nd day air within the continental U.S.

- • repeating gables highlight beautiful elevation
- • large dining room and staircase focus on 2-story entry
- • large private family room is well-integrated with breakfast area and kitchen

- • kitchen furnished with 2 lazy Susans, pantry and counter which wraps into breakfast area with desk
- • master bath has whirlpool tub, open shower and oversized walk-in closet brightened with window seat

- • romance is added to master suite with fantastic bayed window
- • secondary bedrooms share bath with dual lavs and large linen closet
- • bedroom #2 enhanced by volume ceiling and arched window

Rear Elevation

Parade Home Package

available for all plans

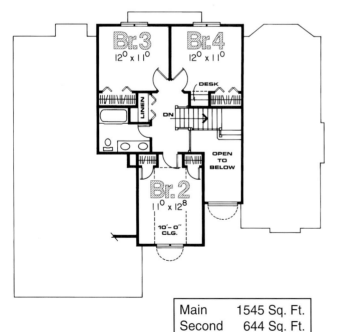

Main	1545 Sq. Ft.
Second	644 Sq. Ft.
Total	2189 Sq. Ft.

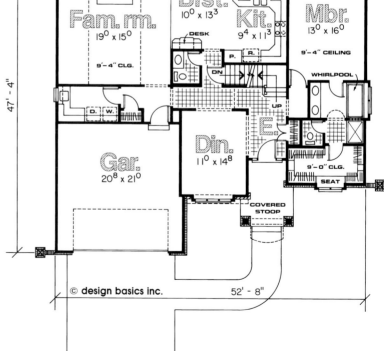

GS1018-21 Maximum

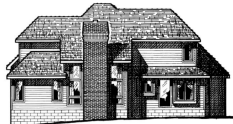

▶ **High quality, erasable, reproducible vellums**
▶ **Shipped via 2nd day air within the continental U.S.**

- dining room with boxed window and hutch space open to volume entry
- view from entry reveals volume great room's handsome brick fireplace flanked by large windows
- centrally located main floor powder bath

- island kitchen with lazy Susan, 2 pantries, built-in desk and breakfast area with bright boxed windows
- garage accesses home through conveniently located laundry room

- master suite with special ceiling detail includes dressing/bath area with his and her vanity, walk-in closet and 2-person whirlpool tub
- upstairs landing overlooks great room and entry area

Rear Elevation

Version of GS1071-20 the "Maxwell" as seen on page 51.

PROMOTIONAL LICENSE • Black and White, Camera-Ready Artwork of the home plan FREE with any plan purchase to assist you in advertising the home.

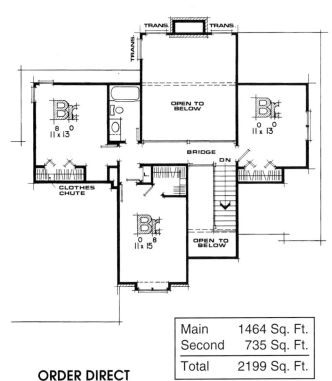

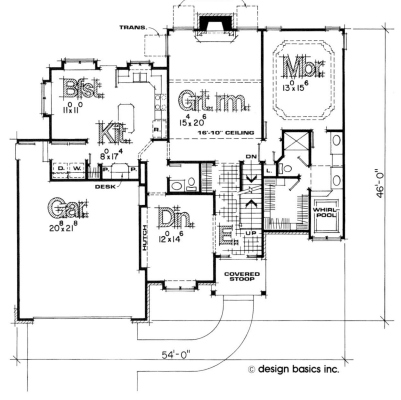

© design basics inc.

Main	1464 Sq. Ft.
Second	735 Sq. Ft.
Total	2199 Sq. Ft.

ORDER DIRECT
7:00-6:00 Mon.-Fri. CST
800-947-PLAN

design basics inc.®
HOME PLAN DESIGN SERVICE

TWO
STORY
HOMES

GS2699-18 Benson

PRICE CODE **18**

• brick and glass block accents, plus wood-railed porch create front elevation that's contemporary, yet nostalgic
• dining room offers ample space for formal dinner occasions

• family room with raised hearth fireplace provides open feeling and endless decorating options
• kitchen features 2 lazy Susans, centrally-placed range and handy snack bar

• master bath is conveniently laid out with separate vanities
• master bedroom boasts 9-foot-high ceiling and spacious dressing area
• well-appointed master bath includes step-up whirlpool and plant shelf

Rear Elevation

ORIGINAL **C** DRAFT
ALL DESIGN BASICS PLANS HAVE BEEN REGISTERED WITH THE U.S. COPYRIGHT OFFICE

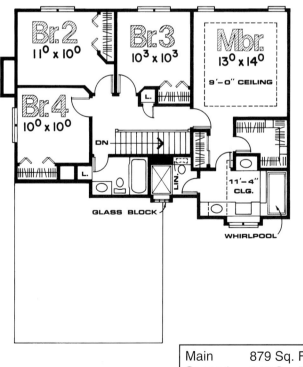

Br.2 11⁰ x 10⁰
Br.3 10³ x 10³
Mbr. 13⁰ x 14⁰ — 9'-0" CEILING
Br.4 10⁰ x 10⁰
DN
L.
LIN.
11'-4" CLG.
GLASS BLOCK
WHIRLPOOL

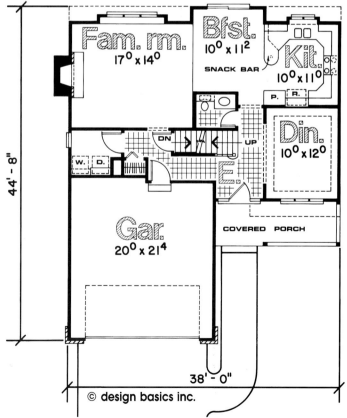

Fam. rm. 17⁰ x 14⁰
Bfst. 10⁰ x 11² — SNACK BAR
Kit. 10⁰ x 11⁰
P. R.
DN
UP
Din. 10⁰ x 12⁰
E.
W. D.
Gar. 20⁰ x 21⁴
COVERED PORCH
44'-8"
38'-0"

© design basics inc.

Main	879 SQ. FT.
Second	945 SQ. FT.
Total	1824 SQ. FT.

design basics inc.®
HOME PLAN DESIGN SERVICE

PRICE CODE
GS2547-18 Jasper

▶ High quality, erasable, reproducible vellums
▶ Shipped via 2nd day air within the continental U.S.

- attractive 2-story home with brick accenting front elevation
- handsome wood floor joins the family room, dinette and kitchen
- family room is highlighted by a fireplace and useful built-in bookcase

- dinette is a bright point featuring delightful bayed windows
- formal entertaining options multiply as dining room opens to volume living room

- impressive double doors lead to a distinctive master bedroom distinguished by his and her walk-in closets
- French doors open to luxurious master bath featuring dual vanities, large whirlpool and separate shower area

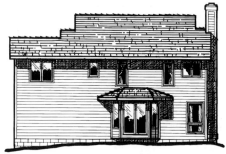

Rear Elevation

Version of GS2559-16 the "Archer" as seen on page 73 of Homes of Distinction.

Parade Home Package
available for all plans

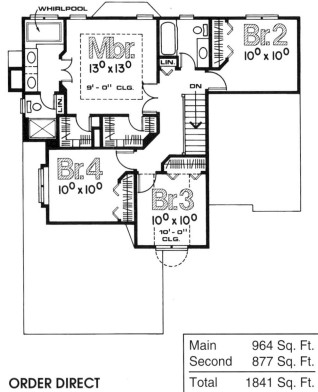

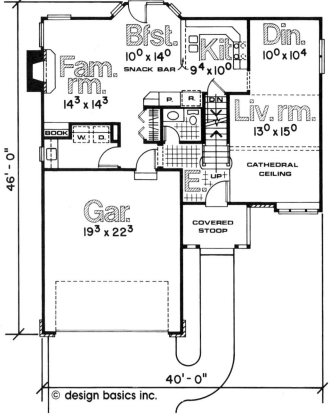

© design basics inc.

ORDER DIRECT
7:00-6:00 Mon.-Fri. CST
800-947-PLAN

Main	964 Sq. Ft.
Second	877 Sq. Ft.
Total	1841 Sq. Ft.

design basics inc.
HOME PLAN DESIGN SERVICE

GS1868-18 Somerset

PRICE CODE **18**

> ▶ High quality, erasable, reproducible vellums
> ▶ Shipped via 2nd day air within the continental U.S.

- appealing porch graces elevation
- light and airy 2-story entrance with large guest closet and plant shelf above
- formal dining room encourages intimate meals or entertaining options
- row of picture/awning windows showcase great room with striking fireplace
- expansive island kitchen and bayed breakfast area with open view to back yard
- secondary bedrooms afford comfort and privacy
- lovely master suite with tiered ceiling includes compartmented bath, two walk-in closets, dual lavs and whirlpool tub

Rear Elevation

PROMOTIONAL LICENSE • PROMOTIONAL LICENSE

Black and White, Camera-Ready Artwork of the home plan FREE with any plan purchase to assist you in advertising the home.

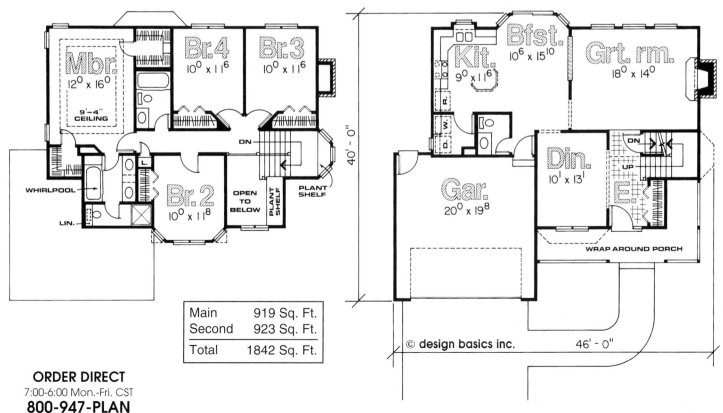

Main	919 Sq. Ft.
Second	923 Sq. Ft.
Total	1842 Sq. Ft.

ORDER DIRECT
7:00-6:00 Mon.-Fri. CST

800-947-PLAN

VISA MasterCard AMERICAN EXPRESS Cards DISCOVER NOVUS

design basics inc.®
HOME PLAN DESIGN SERVICE

GS2100-18 Fenton

PRICE CODE

Gold Seal ™
HOME PLANS

▶ **High quality, erasable, reproducible vellums**
▶ **Shipped via 2nd day air within the continental U.S.**

- quaint front porch
- staircase and formal volume living room seen from entry
- dining room open to living room for entertaining ease

- pantry, lazy Susan and window above sink in kitchen
- bright bayed dinette overlooks family room
- step down into family room with handsome fireplace and wall of windows out the back
- powder bath centrally located

- angles add interest to bedroom #3
- private master bedroom with boxed ceiling features walk-in closet and pampering dressing area with double vanity and whirlpool on angle under window

Rear Elevation

Version of GS2154-19 the "Galvin" as seen on page 89, GS2156-20 the "Graham" as seen on page 102 and GS2157-23 the "Lauderdale" as seen on page 76 of Homes of Elegance.

ALL PLANS *Customizable*

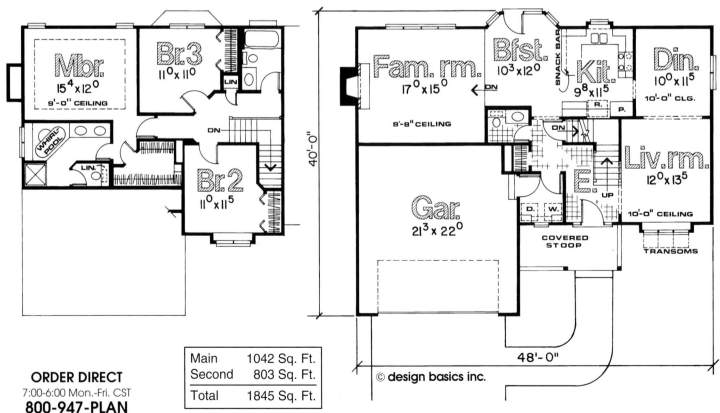

© design basics inc.

ORDER DIRECT
7:00-6:00 Mon.-Fri. CST
800-947-PLAN

Main	1042 Sq. Ft.
Second	803 Sq. Ft.
Total	1845 Sq. Ft.

VISA MasterCard AMERICAN EXPRESS Cards DISCOVER NOVUS

design basics inc. ®
HOME PLAN DESIGN SERVICE

GS1752-18 Lancaster
PRICE CODE

▶ High quality, erasable, reproducible vellums
▶ Shipped via 2nd day air within the continental U.S.

- 2-story entry with large coat closet and plant shelf above
- strategically located staircase
- great room with many windows
- island kitchen with boxed window over sink

- large bayed dinette
- convenient powder bath location
- main floor laundry
- volume ceiling and arched window in front bedroom

- pleasant secondary bedrooms with interesting angles
- large master suite with his and her walk-in closets, corner windows and bath area featuring double vanity and whirlpool bath

Rear Elevation

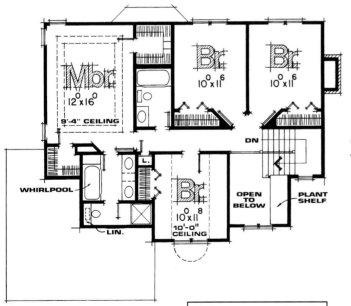

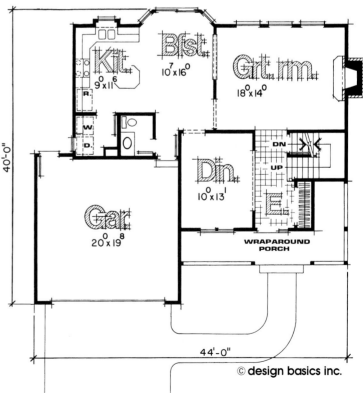

Main	919 Sq. Ft.
Second	927 Sq. Ft.
Total	1846 Sq. Ft.

© design basics inc.

ORDER DIRECT
7:00-6:00 Mon.-Fri. CST
800-947-PLAN

HOME PLAN DESIGN SERVICE

PRICE CODE

GS2950-18 Herald

▶ **High quality, erasable, reproducible vellums**
▶ **Shipped via 2nd day air within the continental U.S.**

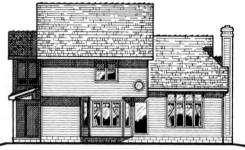

Gold Seal ™
HOME PLANS

- parlor off entry has dining room option and French doors to family room
- back yard door shared by large family room and bayed breakfast area with pantry

- island kitchen open to breakfast area features a second pantry and 2 lazy Susans
- desirable mud porch allows side yard access to utility area with $^1/_2$ bath and laundry room

- back stairs lead to well-planned second level
- secondary bedrooms share hall bath
- amenities abound in master suite with whirlpool bath, built-in linen cabinet and ample walk-in closet off dressing area

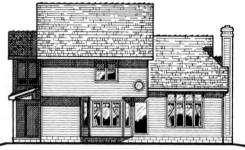

Rear Elevation

PROMOTIONAL LICENSE • PROMOTIONAL LICENSE • PROMOTIONAL LICENSE • PROMOTIONAL LICENSE

Black and White, Camera-Ready Artwork of the home plan FREE with any plan purchase to assist you in advertising the home.

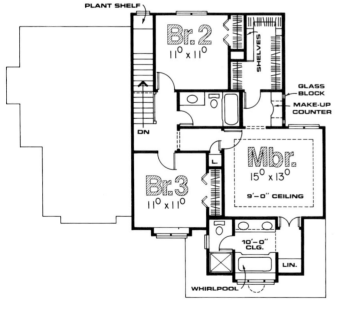

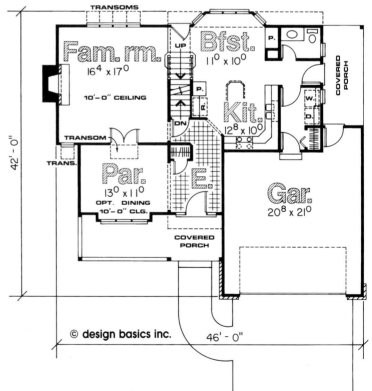

© design basics inc.

Main	972 Sq. Ft.
Second	877 Sq. Ft.
Total	1849 Sq. Ft.

ORDER DIRECT
7:00-6:00 Mon.-Fri. CST
800-947-PLAN

HOME PLAN DESIGN SERVICE

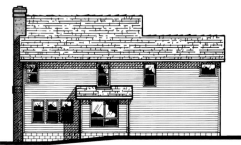

▶ High quality, erasable, reproducible vellums
▶ Shipped via 2nd day air within the continental U.S.

- front porch brings charming twist to this economical elevation
- oak flooring adds elegance to entry and dining room
- bright windows and fireplace compliment relaxed family room

- breakfast area conveniently accesses both backyard and garage
- kitchen enhanced with peninsula snack bar
- organized laundry and powder room off kitchen

- master suite reveals dual sink vanity and romantic corner whirlpool tub
- bedroom #3 offers walk-in closet
- extra storage space in deep garage

Rear Elevation

Version of GS3459-15 the "Jamestown" as seen on page 67 of Homes of Distinction.

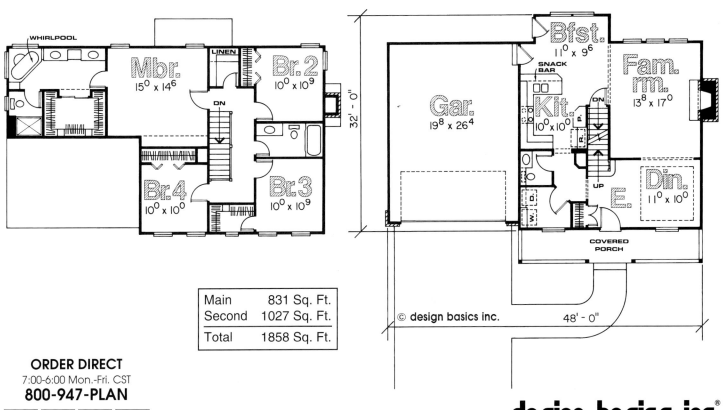

Main	831 Sq. Ft.
Second	1027 Sq. Ft.
Total	1858 Sq. Ft.

© design basics inc.

ORDER DIRECT
7:00-6:00 Mon.-Fri. CST
800-947-PLAN

VISA MasterCard AMERICAN EXPRESS Cards DUCOVER NOVUS

design basics inc.
HOME PLAN DESIGN SERVICE

GS2966-18 Liberty

PRICE CODE 18

▶ High quality, erasable, reproducible vellums
▶ Shipped via 2nd day air within the continental U.S.

- charming colonial has prominent entry
- great room, off 2-story entry, offers views to covered porch and bayed dinette
- island kitchen with pantry and lazy Susan has convenient access to dining room, garage and efficient laundry

- large formal dining provides impressive view from entry
- on second level cased openings add privacy for bedrooms

- secondary bedrooms share hall bath
- master suite includes well-lit bedroom with cathedral ceiling and whirlpool bath with generous walk-in closet, open shower and dual lavs

Rear Elevation

Version of GS2963-19 the "Columbus" as seen on page 83.

Parade Home Package

available for all plans

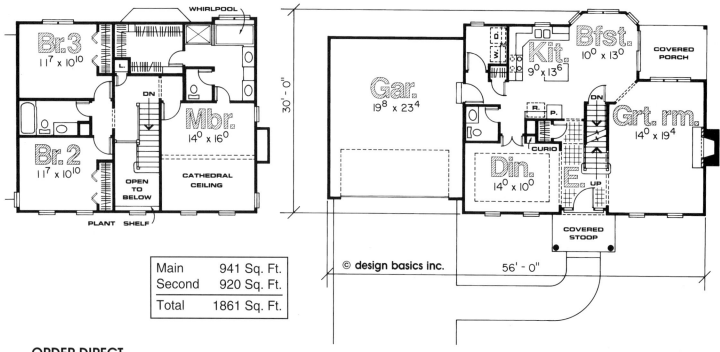

Main	941 Sq. Ft.
Second	920 Sq. Ft.
Total	1861 Sq. Ft.

ORDER DIRECT
7:00-6:00 Mon.-Fri. CST
800-947-PLAN

GS746-18 Monroe
PRICE CODE 18

Gold Seal
HOME PLANS ™

- covered front porch
- step-down from entry into volume living room open to formal dining room with vaulted ceiling
- window in compartmented main-floor laundry area
- awning window centers above bookcase in family room with fireplace
- well-planned kitchen with lazy Susan, pantry and many cabinets is open to breakfast area
- cathedral ceiling in master bedroom
- skylit dressing area and compartmented stool in master bath, plus walk-in closet
- volume ceiling in front bedroom with beautiful arched window

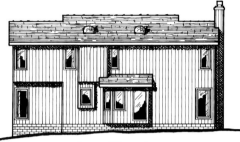

Rear Elevation

Version of GS846-20 the "Ardmore" as seen on page 95.

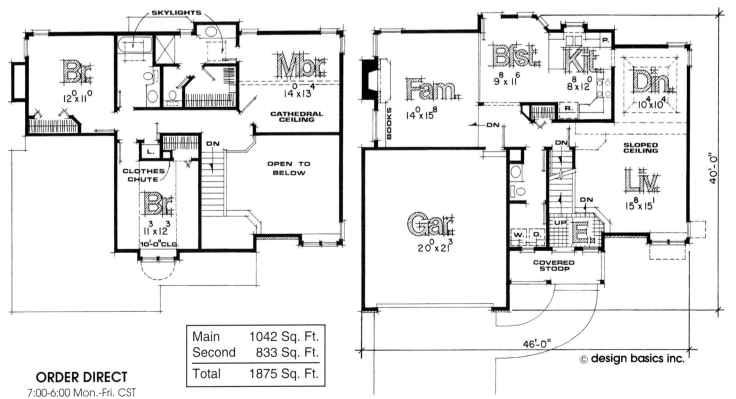

SKYLIGHTS

Br
12⁰ x 11⁰

Mbr
14 x 13
CATHEDRAL CEILING

OPEN TO BELOW

L.
CLOTHES CHUTE

DN

Br
11 x 12
10'-0" CLG.

Fam
14⁰ x 15⁸

Bfst
9⁸ x 11⁶

Kit
8 x 12

Dn
10⁴ x 10⁴

BOOKS

DN

DN

SLOPED CEILING

Lv
15⁸ x 15¹

Gar
20⁰ x 23

UP

W. D.

COVERED STOOP

40'-0"

46'-0"

© design basics inc.

Main	1042 SQ. FT.
Second	833 SQ. FT.
Total	1875 SQ. FT.

design basics inc.®
HOME PLAN DESIGN SERVICE

GS2948-18 Peyton

PRICE CODE

Gold Seal™
HOME PLANS

▶ **High quality, erasable, reproducible vellums**
▶ **Shipped via 2nd day air within the continental U.S.**

- covered porch paired with cedar shakes and stone create a charming elevation
- 2-story entry captures picturesque views of elegant colonnade framing entry to great room and open U-stairs with plant ledge above landing

- formal dining room, open to great room and entry, has direct access from kitchen
- bayed dinette open to great kitchen featuring large pantry, 2 lazy Susans and snack bar
- spacious garage has storage area

- upstairs hallway overlooking entry leads to secondary bedrooms sharing sun-lit bath
- master suite highlighted by vaulted ceiling and whirlpool bath with dramatic angled walls, sloped ceiling and spacious walk-in closet

Rear Elevation

Version of GS3028-20 the "Ferguson" as seen on page 96.

ALL PLANS *Customizable*

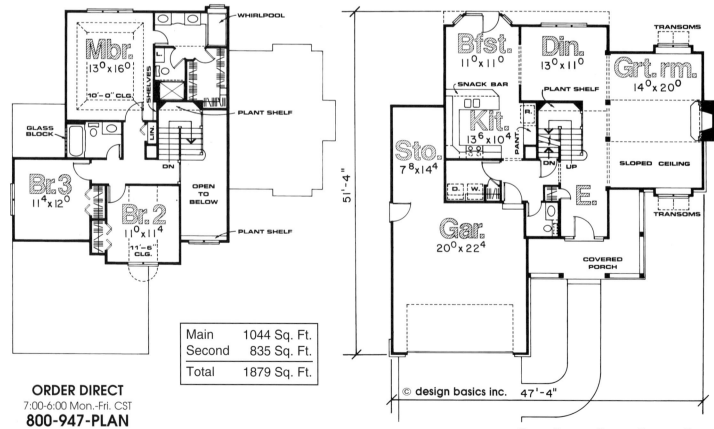

Main	1044 Sq. Ft.
Second	835 Sq. Ft.
Total	1879 Sq. Ft.

ORDER DIRECT

7:00-6:00 Mon.-Fri. CST

800-947-PLAN

VISA MasterCard AMERICAN EXPRESS Cards DISCOVER NOVUS

design basics inc®
HOME PLAN DESIGN SERVICE

GS2305-18 Austin

PRICE CODE

► High quality, erasable, reproducible vellums
► Shipped via 2nd day air within the continental U.S.

- elegant lines of this two-story elevation give additional enticement
- dramatic tiled entry hall leads conveniently to all areas
- adjacent living and dining areas enhance every entertaining pursuit

- kitchen and bayed breakfast area located strategically to serve both the formal dining area and the family room
- bright picture window and lovely raised hearth fireplace highlight family room

- second level arrangement offers unique privacy to secondary bedrooms and gives seclusion to master suite
- sumptuous master suite features two closets and a sunlit whirlpool tub and dressing area

Rear Elevation

Version of GS2308-17 the "Juniper" as seen on page 85 of Homes of Distinction.

Parade Home Package
available for all plans

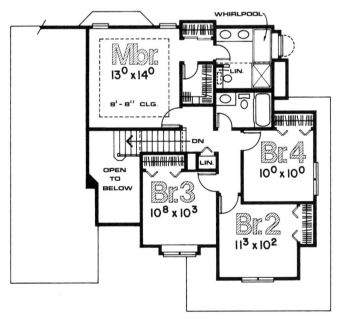

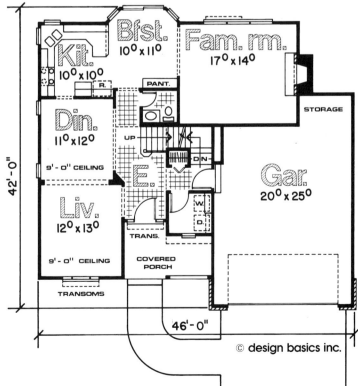

© design basics inc.

Main	1032 Sq. Ft.
Second	865 Sq. Ft.
Total	1897 Sq. Ft.

ORDER DIRECT
7:00-6:00 Mon.-Fri. CST

800-947-PLAN

► **High quality, erasable, reproducible vellums**
► **Shipped via 2nd day air within the continental U.S.**

- suitable for narrower lots
- view from entry to see-thru fireplace and wall of windows in great room
- thoughtful traffic patterns
- strategic powder bath location

- bayed breakfast area into island kitchen with fireplace and built-in pantry
- staircase open to entry
- plant ledge above entry closet
- clothes chute and double lavs in hall bath

- French doors into master bedroom with vaulted ceiling and walk-in closet
- double lavs and whirlpool tub in master bath
- generous secondary bedrooms

Rear Elevation

PROMOTIONAL LICENSE • PROMOTIONAL LICENSE

Black and White, Camera-Ready Artwork of the home plan FREE with any plan purchase to assist you in advertising the home.

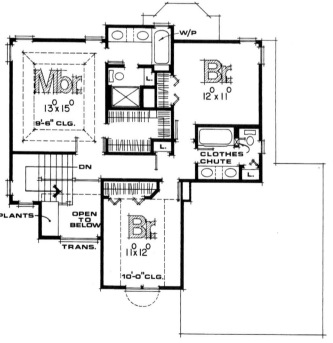

Mbr
13⁰ x 15⁰
9'-6" CLG.

Br
12⁰ x 11⁰

W/P

CLOTHES CHUTE

DN

PLANTS

OPEN TO BELOW

TRANS.

Br
11 x 12⁰
10'-0" CLG.

Bfst
10⁰ x 10⁰

Grt. rm.
18⁴ x 15⁰

Kit.
16⁰ x 12⁷

R.
P.
W. D.

STORAGE

DN
UP

COVERED STOOP

Dn
12⁰ x 13⁰

HUTCH

Gar
19⁴ x 20⁴

45'-0"

44'-0"

© design basics inc.

ORDER DIRECT
7:00-6:00 Mon.-Fri. CST
800-947-PLAN

Main	1012 Sq. Ft.
Second	900 Sq. Ft.
Total	1912 Sq. Ft.

design basics inc.
HOME PLAN DESIGN SERVICE

GS3386-19 Mansell

PRICE CODE

- High quality, erasable, reproducible vellums
- Shipped via 2nd day air within the continental U.S.

- gingerbread comes alive in elevation packed with traditional flair
- large living room with 10-foot ceiling and bayed windows is seen from entry
- both kitchen and living room benefit from nearby dining room with 10-foot ceiling

- snack bar, wrapping counters and two lazy Susans in kitchen
- gigantic sunken family room fosters activity with its fireplace and sunny windows
- bayed breakfast area has access to backyard

- master suite features 9-foot boxed ceiling, bayed windows and walk-in closet
- whirlpool and dual lavs in master bath
- bayed windows and 10-foot ceiling highlight bedroom #2

Rear Elevation

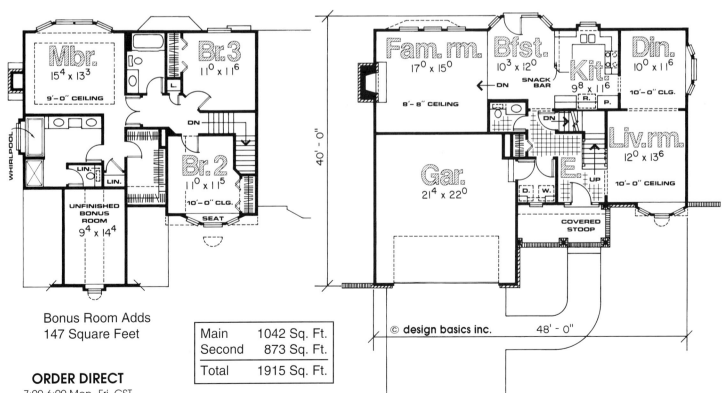

Bonus Room Adds
147 Square Feet

Main	1042 Sq. Ft.
Second	873 Sq. Ft.
Total	1915 Sq. Ft.

ORDER DIRECT
7:00-6:00 Mon.-Fri. CST
800-947-PLAN

GS2235-19 Albany

PRICE CODE

Gold Seal HOME PLANS

▸ **High quality, erasable, reproducible vellums**
▸ **Shipped via 2nd day air within the continental U.S.**

- inviting covered porch
- interesting staircase with landing in volume entry
- abundant windows throughout
- 10-foot ceiling and handsome fireplace in great room

- island counter, pantry and desk in open kitchen/dinette area
- kitchen conveniently accesses laundry room
- upstairs landing overlooks entry below

- beautiful arched window under volume ceiling in bedroom #2
- master suite features pampering dressing area with double vanity, compartmented stool and shower plus whirlpool under window

Rear Elevation

Version of GS2244-17 the "Standley" as seen on page 79 of Homes of Distinction.

Parade Home Package
available for all plans

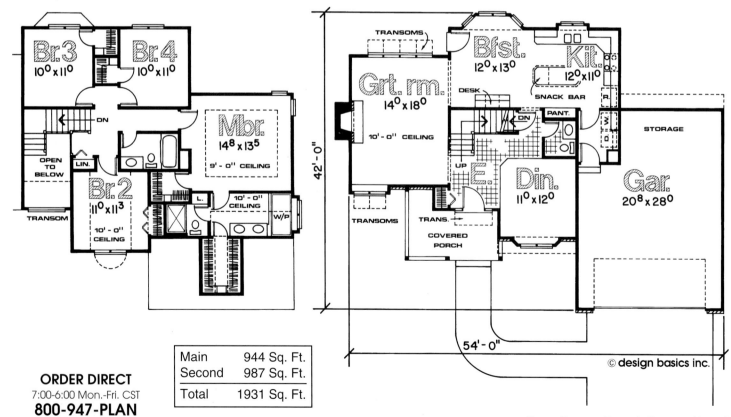

© design basics inc.

ORDER DIRECT
7:00-6:00 Mon.-Fri. CST
800-947-PLAN

VISA MasterCard American Express Cards Discover Novus

Main	944 Sq. Ft.
Second	987 Sq. Ft.
Total	1931 Sq. Ft.

design basics inc.®
HOME PLAN DESIGN SERVICE

Gold Seal HOME PLANS ™

▶ High quality, erasable, reproducible vellums
▶ Shipped via 2nd day air within the continental U.S.

- spectacular entry and great window details create sophisticated elevation
- 14-foot-wide formal dining room and great room surround 2-story entry
- angled cased opening connects great room and bayed dinette

- patio door in large dinette accesses desirable, private covered porch
- island kitchen with lazy Susan and pantry has direct access to dining room through elegant French doors

- on second level, 3 secondary bedrooms are serviced by hall bath with dual lavs
- well-planned whirlpool bath, walk-in closet with recessed doors and boxed 9-foot-high ceiling creates deluxe master suite

Rear Elevation

Version of GS2966-18 the "Liberty" as seen on page 76.

PROMOTIONAL LICENSE • Black and White, Camera-Ready Artwork of the home plan FREE with any plan purchase to assist you in advertising the home.

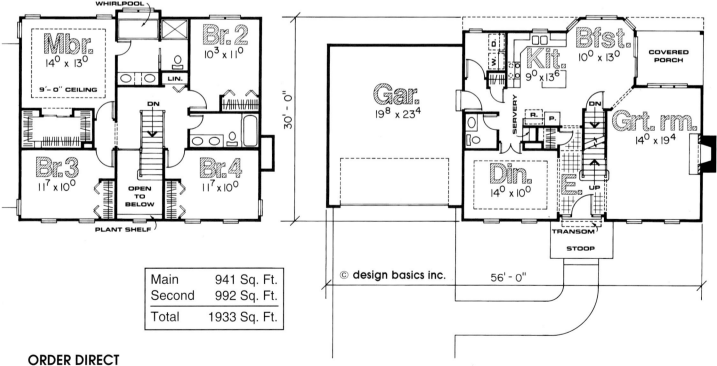

Main	941 Sq. Ft.
Second	992 Sq. Ft.
Total	1933 Sq. Ft.

© design basics inc.

ORDER DIRECT
7:00-6:00 Mon.-Fri. CST
800-947-PLAN

design basics inc. ®
HOME PLAN DESIGN SERVICE

PRICE CODE

GS3568-19 Melrose

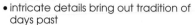

▶ **High quality, erasable, reproducible vellums**
▶ **Shipped via 2nd day air within the continental U.S.**

- intricate details bring out tradition of days past
- window seat and volume ceiling upon entry
- parlor creates elegant atmosphere and is flexible as dining room

- kitchen/breakfast area offers island counter, boxed windows and lazy Susan
- view of backyard can be seen from spacious family room through lovely windows
- back staircase location is convenient to living areas of the home

- French doors reveal 9'-0" ceiling, whirlpool tub and plant shelf in master suite
- bedroom #2 has 10'-0" ceiling and shares full bath with bedroom #3
- optional bonus room on second floor

Rear Elevation

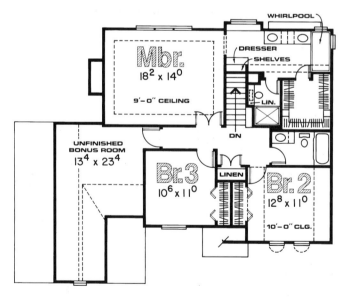

Bonus Room Adds
260 Square Feet

Main	995 SQ. FT.
Second	952 SQ. FT.
Total	1947 SQ. FT.

ORDER DIRECT
7:00-6:00 Mon.-Fri. CST
800-947-PLAN

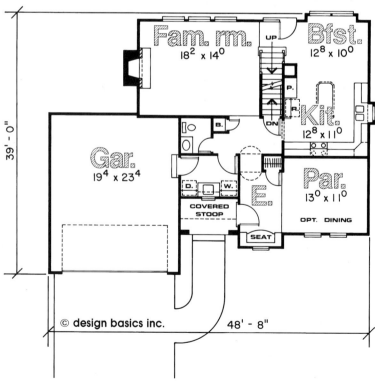

© design basics inc.

GS2648-19 Cyprus

PRICE CODE 19

▶ High quality, erasable, reproducible vellums
▶ Shipped via 2nd day air within the continental U.S.

GoldSeal ™
HOME PLANS

- brilliant design character captures great livability in this striking 2-story home
- whether used as office, library, or as formal living room, parlor with privacy is valuable design

- T-shaped staircase smooths traffic flow
- well-appointed kitchen is just steps away from dinette and dining room
- integrated design of family room, dinette and kitchen capitalize on comfortable family living and easy entertaining

- charming window seat complements comfortable master bedroom
- all desired amenities such as walk-in closet, dual lavs and whirlpool are featured in master bath

Rear Elevation

Version of GS2638-21 the "Linden" as seen on page 104.

Parade Home Package
available for all plans

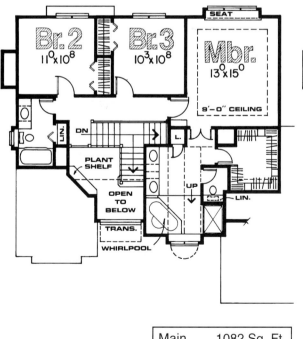

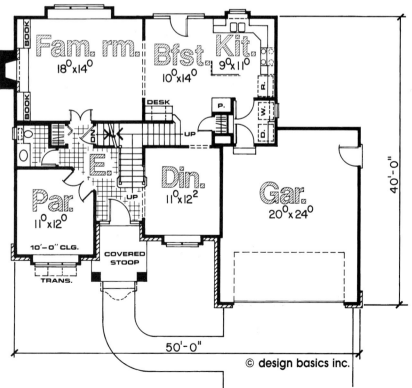

© design basics inc.

Main	1082 Sq. Ft.
Second	869 Sq. Ft.
Total	1951 Sq. Ft.

ORDER DIRECT
7:00-6:00 Mon.-Fri. CST
800-947-PLAN

design basics inc. ®
HOME PLAN DESIGN SERVICE

GS852-19 Vincennes

PRICE CODE

Gold Seal HOME PLANS™

- energy efficient airlock entry with coat closet
- wrapping staircase open to spacious volume great room with bookcases, fireplace and large windows to the back
- phone booth at base of staircase

- gourmet kitchen includes 2 lazy Susans, pantry and snack bar to serve adjacent sun space and dining area
- garage accesses home through laundry/mud room with coat closet and iron-a-way

- master suite features vaulted ceiling, 2 closets, his and her vanities and whirlpool tub
- secondary bedrooms share hall bath served by 2 linen closets
- upstairs landing overlooks great room

Rear Elevation

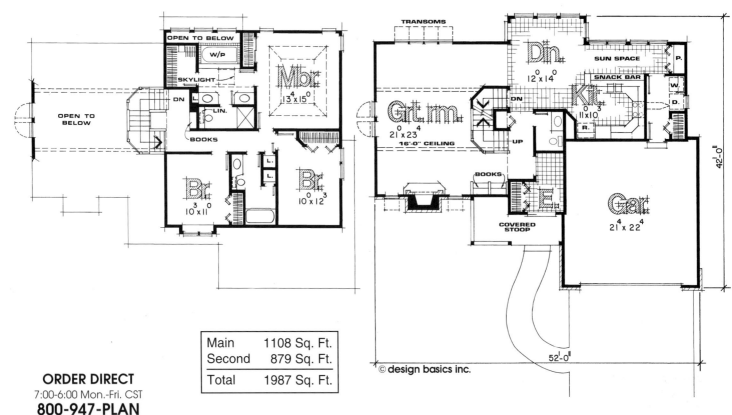

Main	1108 Sq. Ft.
Second	879 Sq. Ft.
Total	1987 Sq. Ft.

© design basics inc.

design basics inc
HOME PLAN DESIGN SERVICE

GS3384-**19** Frederick

PRICE CODE

▶ High quality, erasable, reproducible vellums
▶ Shipped via 2nd day air within the continental U.S.

- exterior details combine to evoke emotion
- living room boasts 10-foot ceiling and boxed window
- dining room openly connected to living room - perfect for formal gatherings

- wrapping counters and corner sink in kitchen open to bayed breakfast area
- laundry room and back hall closet convenient features near garage entry
- master bedroom with boxed ceiling and walk-in offers perfect place to retreat

- pampering master bath presents whirlpool tub under arched window plus separate shower
- bedroom #2 has large walk-in closet

Rear Elevation

Main	1140 Sq. Ft.
Second	852 Sq. Ft.
Total	1992 Sq. Ft.

ORDER DIRECT
7:00-6:00 Mon.-Fri. CST

800-947-PLAN

© design basics inc.

design basics inc.®
HOME PLAN DESIGN SERVICE

GS2315-19 Harrisburg

▸ **High quality, erasable, reproducible vellums**
▸ **Shipped via 2nd day air within the continental U.S.**

- stately front elevation gives dynamic impact
- dramatic French doors connect formal living room and family room
- family room enhanced by raised hearth fireplace and bayed conversation area

- gourmet kitchen/breakfast area profits from extra-large pantry, two lazy Susans and patio door to the rear yard
- attractive stairway leads to second floor corridor with bookcase and large linen closet

- arrangement of secondary bedrooms gives privacy but remain within easy access to a roomy bath
- master suite enjoys volume ceiling, built-in bookcase and luxurious compartmented bath/dressing area

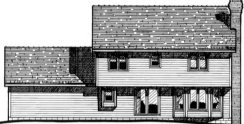

Rear Elevation

Version of GS2401-20 the "Curtiss" as seen on page 94 and GS2316-23 the "Franklin" as seen on page 82 of Homes of Elegance.

Parade Home Package
available for all plans

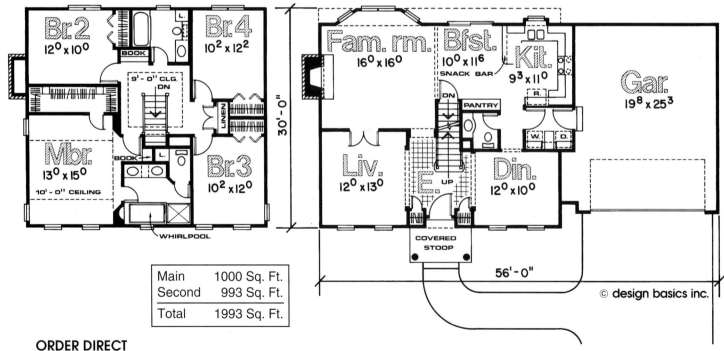

Main	1000 Sq. Ft.
Second	993 Sq. Ft.
Total	1993 Sq. Ft.

© design basics inc.

ORDER DIRECT
7:00-6:00 Mon.-Fri. CST
800-947-PLAN

GS2154-19 Galvin
PRICE CODE

▶ High quality, erasable, reproducible vellums
▶ Shipped via 2nd day air within the continental U.S.

- volume living room seen from entry with beautiful boxed window
- formal dining room open to living room for versatility
- informal and formal areas well segregated for comfortable living

- step down into large family room with handsome fireplace and wall of windows out to the back
- bayed dinette open to kitchen with snack bar, pantry and 2 lazy Susans

- private master bedroom with formal boxed ceiling
- master dressing area features walk-in closet, double vanity and angled whirlpool under window

Rear Elevation

Version of GS2100-18 the "Fenton" as seen on page 72, GS2156-20 the "Graham" as seen on page 102 and GS2157-23 the "Lauderdale" as seen on page 76 of Homes of Elegance.

PROMOTIONAL LICENSE
Black and White, Camera-Ready Artwork of the home plan FREE with any plan purchase to assist you in advertising the home.

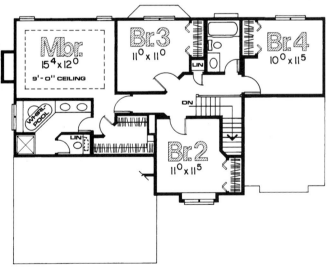

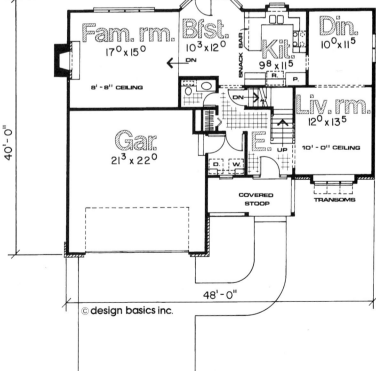

Main	1042 Sq. Ft.
Second	953 Sq. Ft.
Total	1995 Sq. Ft.

ORDER DIRECT
7:00-6:00 Mon.-Fri. CST
800-947-PLAN

design basics inc.®
HOME PLAN DESIGN SERVICE

GS2619-19 Oakbrook

PRICE CODE

- distinctive design personality is complemented by large covered porch with wood railing
- living room is distinguished by warmth of bayed window and French doors leading to family room

- built-in curio cabinet adds interest to formal dining room
- large laundry room provides practical and desirable access from garage, outdoors and kitchen

- well-appointed kitchen with island cook top is planned to save you steps
- family room is perfect for informal gatherings
- secondary bedrooms share comparmented hall bath

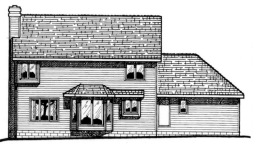

Rear Elevation

Version of GS2618-21 the "Paisley" as seen on page 106.

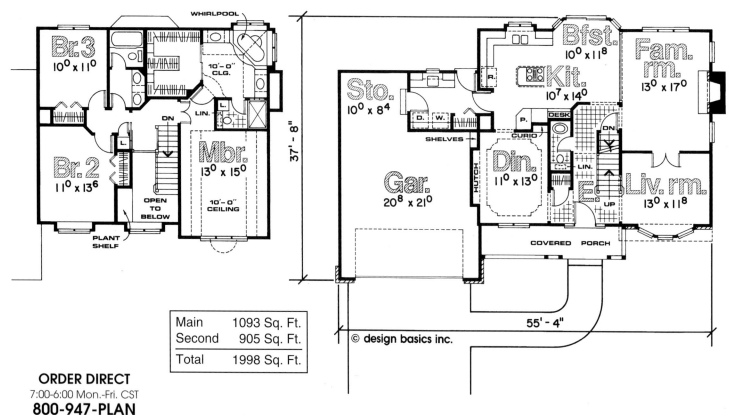

Main	1093 Sq. Ft.
Second	905 Sq. Ft.
Total	1998 Sq. Ft.

ORDER DIRECT
7:00-6:00 Mon.-Fri. CST
800-947-PLAN

design basics inc.®
HOME PLAN DESIGN SERVICE

GS3552-**20** Ballobin

PRICE CODE

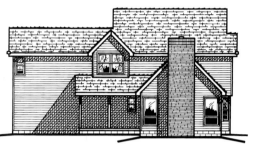

▶ High quality, erasable, reproducible vellums
▶ Shipped via 2nd day air within the continental U.S.

- front elevation captures attention with alluring windows and porch
- dining room opts as formal parlor
- convenient coat closet in oak entry
- front and back covered porches to enjoy outdoors

- abundant counter space serves kitchen
- bayed breakfast area accesses snack bar
- large family room presents cathedral ceiling and windows framing warm fireplace

- French doors reveal 9'-0" boxed ceiling, dual lavs and whirlpool in master suite
- compartmented hall bath with twin lavs serves secondary bedrooms
- bedroom #3 possesses walk-in closet

Rear Elevation

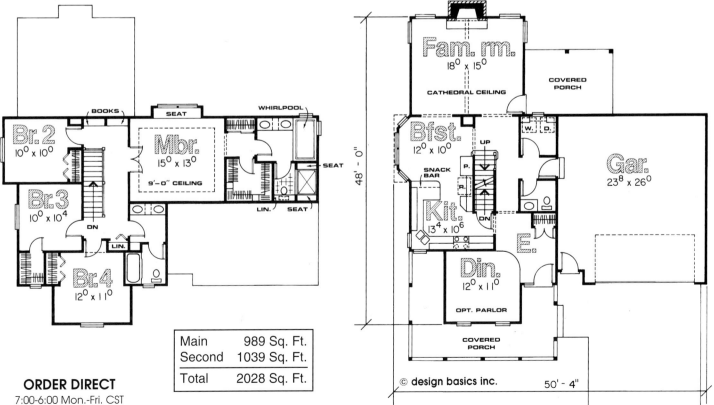

Main	989 SQ. FT.
Second	1039 SQ. FT.
Total	2028 SQ. FT.

ORDER DIRECT
7:00-6:00 Mon.-Fri. CST
800-947-PLAN

© design basics inc.

design basics inc.®
HOME PLAN DESIGN SERVICE

PRICE CODE
GS1769-20 Hampton

▶ **High quality, erasable, reproducible vellums**
▶ **Shipped via 2nd day air within the continental U.S.**

Gold Seal HOME PLANS™

- large hall coat closet and nearby laundry room convenient to garage entrance into home
- volume living room opens to large dining room for entertaining

- efficient kitchen with pantry and planning desk open to bayed dinette
- sunken family room, private from entry, has fireplace and many windows
- central trafficways throughout
- extra storage space in garage

- secondary bedrooms segregated for privacy share skylit hall bath
- large master bedroom with elaborate skylit master bath includes walk-in closet, double vanity and compartmented stool and shower

Rear Elevation

Main	1081	Sq. Ft.
Second	950	Sq. Ft.
Total	2031	Sq. Ft.

© design basics inc.

ORDER DIRECT
7:00-6:00 Mon.-Fri. CST
800-947-PLAN

VISA MasterCard American Express Cards Discover NOVUS

design basics inc.®
HOME PLAN DESIGN SERVICE

GS797-20 Gadsden

PRICE CODE

Gold Seal
HOME PLANS ™

- dining room open to hard-surfaced entry
- French doors open into den with bookcase
- great room includes fireplace, built-in bookcase and large bayed window to the back
- laundry room with closet and hanging rods

- island kitchen includes corner sink, pantry, desk and sunny breakfast area with door to the outside
- master bedroom with vaulted ceiling plus dressing area featuring walk-in closet with mirrored bi-pass doors and window seat

- upstairs landing brightened by skylight
- secondary bedrooms include walk-in closets and share hall bath with window seat
- front bedroom has window seat

Rear Elevation

ALL PLANS *Customizable*

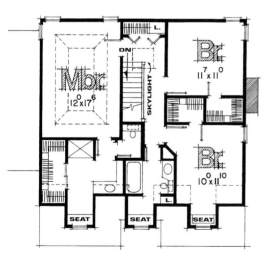

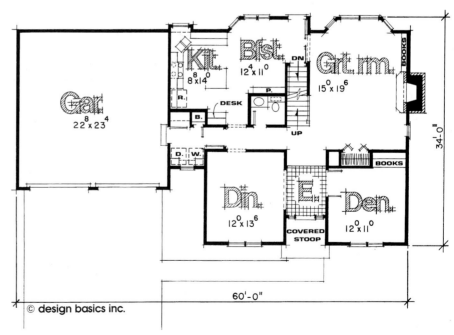

© design basics inc.

60'-0"

34'-0"

Main	1137 Sq. Ft.
Second	917 Sq. Ft.
Total	2054 Sq. Ft.

design basics inc.®
HOME PLAN DESIGN SERVICE

GS2401-20 Curtiss

PRICE CODE

Gold Seal
HOME PLANS ™

- majestically appealing elevation
- entry surveys formal entertaining rooms
- French doors separate living and family rooms
- family room includes warming fireplace and bayed conversation area
- kitchen's design facilitates enjoyment with built-ins and snack bar
- dinette enjoys access to family room and outdoor pursuits
- U-shaped second level hall with bookcase affords privacy to all bedrooms
- secondary bedrooms share bath with extra linen cabinet
- master suite enjoys large walk-in closet and decorative boxed ceiling
- master dressing/bath with dual lavs and arched window above whirlpool tub

Rear Elevation

Version of GS2315-19 the "Harrisburg" as seen on page 88 and GS2316-23 the "Franklin" as seen on page 82 of Homes of Elegance.

Parade Home Package
available for all plans

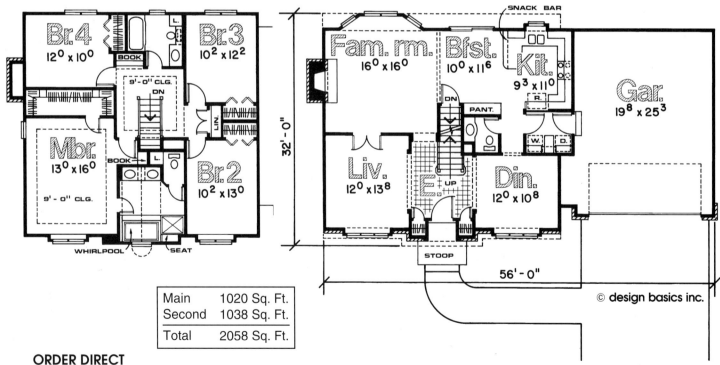

Main	1020 Sq. Ft.
Second	1038 Sq. Ft.
Total	2058 Sq. Ft.

ORDER DIRECT
7:00-6:00 Mon.-Fri. CST
800-947-PLAN

design basics inc.®
HOME PLAN DESIGN SERVICE

GS846-20 Ardmore
PRICE CODE

▶ **High quality, erasable, reproducible vellums**
▶ **Shipped via 2nd day air within the continental U.S.**

- entry offers immediate view of living room with open access to formal dining room for entertaining options
- sunken family room offers built-in bookcase and fireplace

- kitchen features lazy Susan, pantry and window over sink
- wood railing separates sunny breakfast area from family room, enhancing the open feeling

- upstairs balcony overlooks living room below
- master suite includes deluxe dressing/bath area featuring skylight, walk-in closet and private compartmented stool
- secondary bedrooms share skylit hall bath

Rear Elevation

Version of GS746-18 the "Monroe" as seen on page 77.

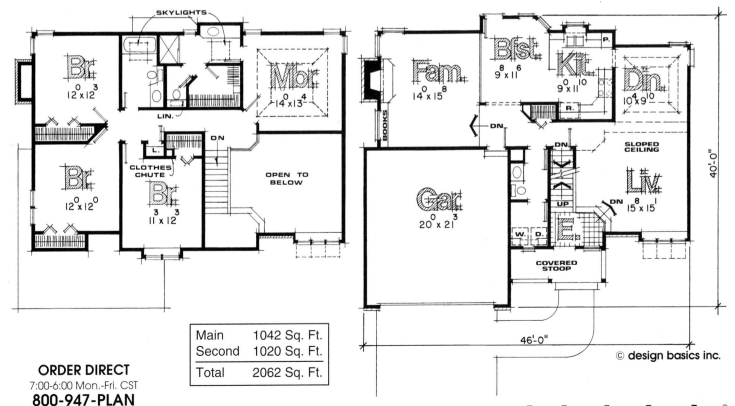

Main	1042 Sq. Ft.
Second	1020 Sq. Ft.
Total	2062 Sq. Ft.

© design basics inc.

ORDER DIRECT
7:00-6:00 Mon.-Fri. CST
800-947-PLAN

design basics inc.®
HOME PLAN DESIGN SERVICE

PRICE CODE

GS3028-20 Ferguson

▶ High quality, erasable, reproducible vellums
▶ Shipped via 2nd day air within the continental U.S.

- built-in bookcase with window between 2 coat closets add charm to entry
- view of colonnade and U-stairs enhance sun-filled great room
- formal dining room well located for entertaining

- peninsula kitchen with large pantry and 2 lazy Susans shares snack bar with bayed dinette
- garage features convenient access to kitchen and laundry room and has extra storage area

- 3 secondary bedrooms share large compartmented bath
- bedroom #2 has walk-in closet
- vaulted ceiling and whirlpool bath with spacious walk-in closet complete lavish master suite

Rear Elevation

Version of GS2948-18 the "Peyton" as seen on page 78.

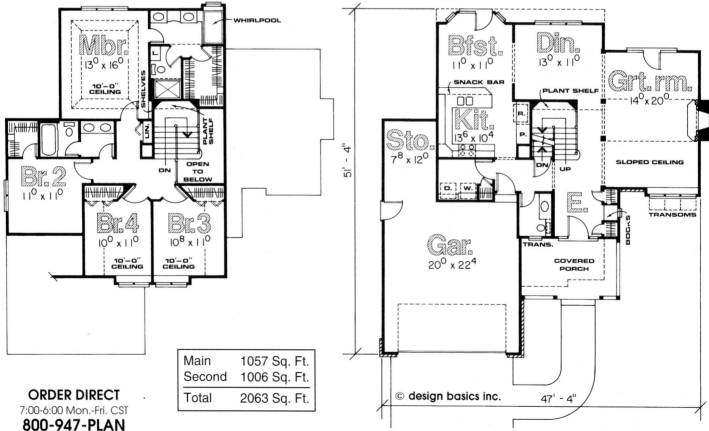

Main	1057 Sq. Ft.
Second	1006 Sq. Ft.
Total	2063 Sq. Ft.

ORDER DIRECT
7:00-6:00 Mon.-Fri. CST
800-947-PLAN

GS1009-**20** Cape Romain

PRICE CODE

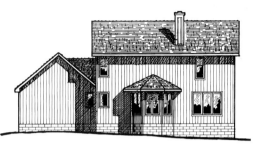

Gold Seal HOME PLANS ™

▸ **High quality, erasable, reproducible vellums**
▸ **Shipped via 2nd day air within the continental U.S.**

- hutch space in formal dining room off entry
- expansive great room with boxed window, see-thru fireplace and bookcases
- wall location provided for optional living room

- kitchen features island counter/snack bar, pantry, desk, fireplace and adjoining gazebo breakfast area
- garage with extra storage area accesses home through laundry/mud room with utility sink

- master bedroom highlighted by volume ceiling and arched transom window
- master bath includes walk-in closet, his and her vanities and whirlpool tub
- secondary bedrooms share convenient hall bath

Rear Elevation

Parade Home Package
available for all plans

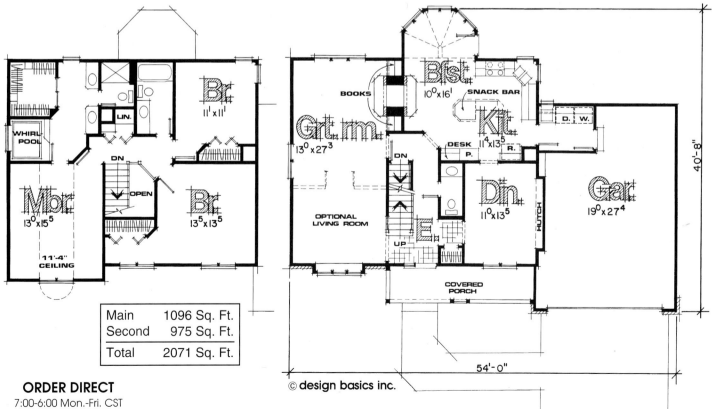

© design basics inc.

Main	1096 Sq. Ft.	
Second	975 Sq. Ft.	
Total	2071 Sq. Ft.	

ORDER DIRECT
7:00-6:00 Mon.-Fri. CST
800-947-PLAN

design basics inc. ®
HOME PLAN DESIGN SERVICE

GS1870-20 Bristol

PRICE CODE

▶ High quality, erasable, reproducible vellums
▶ Shipped via 2nd day air within the continental U.S.

- charming porch and arched windows of elevation allude to elegance within
- parlor with large bayed window and sloped ceiling harks back to simpler life
- formal dining area open to parlor invites entertaining with ease from kitchen

- bright kitchen and bayed breakfast area features wrapping counters, pantry and desk
- step down into expansive gathering room with fireplace and abundant windows

- ample secondary bedrooms share nearby skylit bath
- indulging master bedroom with skylit dressing area, dual lavs, whirlpool tub and large walk-in closet

Rear Elevation

PROMOTIONAL LICENSE • PROMOTIONAL LICENSE

Black and White, Camera-Ready Artwork of the home plan FREE with any plan purchase to assist you in advertising the home.

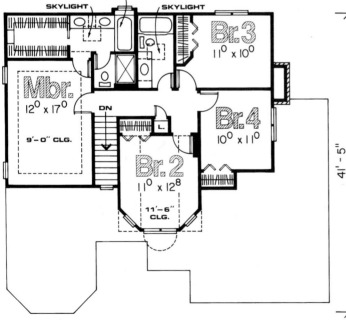

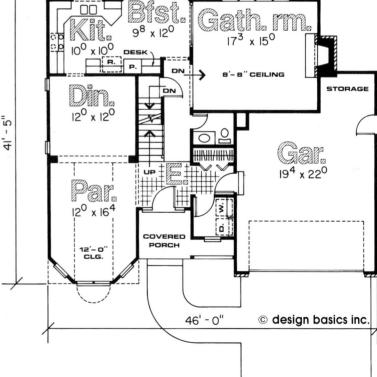

Main	1113 Sq. Ft.
Second	965 Sq. Ft.
Total	2078 Sq. Ft.

ORDER DIRECT
7:00-6:00 Mon.-Fri. CST
800-947-PLAN

design basics inc.®
HOME PLAN DESIGN SERVICE

GS2217-20 Yorke

Gold Seal™
HOME PLANS

- 2-story entry open to interesting staircase and formal dining room with boxed window and hutch space
- great room with large windows, entertainment center and see-thru fireplace

- hearth room takes advantage of see-thru fireplace
- island counter, desk and pantry in kitchen open to bayed dinette
- closet for garage entrance
- window in laundry room

- vaulted ceiling and unique angle into walk-in closet and dressing area make this a special master suite
- irresistible oval whirlpool under arched window and his and her vanities in master bath/dressing area

Rear Elevation

ALL PLANS *Customizable*

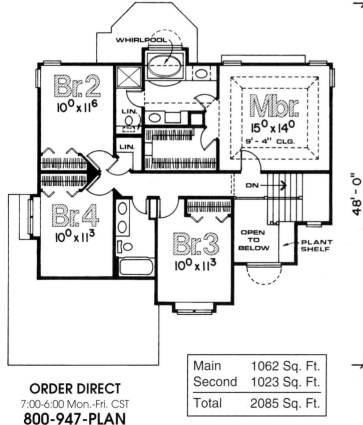

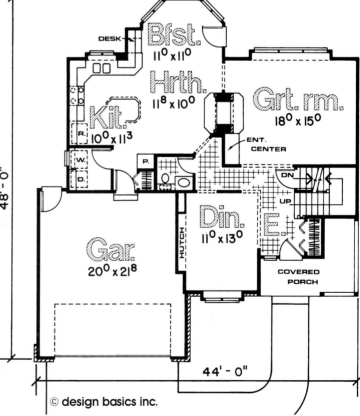

© design basics inc.

Main	1062 Sq. Ft.
Second	1023 Sq. Ft.
Total	2085 Sq. Ft.

design basics inc.®
HOME PLAN DESIGN SERVICE

PRICE CODE

GS1179-**20** Sawyer

▶ **High quality, erasable, reproducible vellums**
▶ **Shipped via 2nd day air within the continental U.S.**

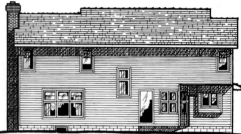

GoldSeal™
HOME PLANS

- main level footage optimized and second level footage maximized
- private door onto spacious wrap-around porch from kitchen
- large kitchen includes pantry, island counter, roll-top desk and lazy Susan

- convenient main floor powder bath
- great room opens to staircase at the rear brightened with window on landing
- double doors to large master bedroom
- deluxe master bath area with whirlpool, transom windows and sloped ceiling

- laundry room with soaking sink on same level as bedrooms
- 3 linen closets on second level
- secondary bedrooms share centrally located bath with double vanity

G. MacDONALD

Rear Elevation

Parade
Home
Package
*available for
all plans*

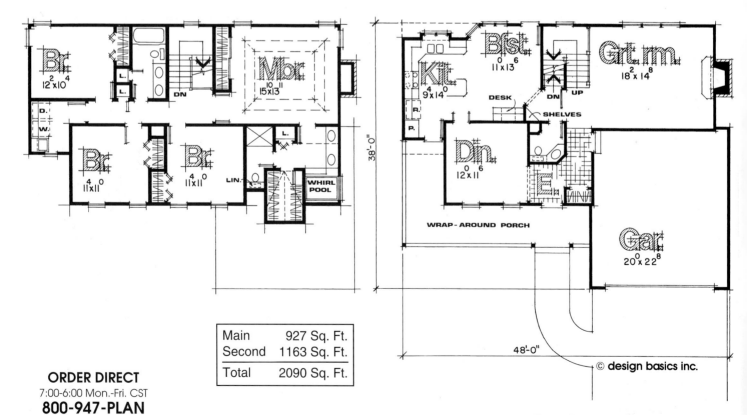

© design basics inc.

Main	927 Sq. Ft.
Second	1163 Sq. Ft.
Total	2090 Sq. Ft.

ORDER DIRECT
7:00-6:00 Mon.-Fri. CST
800-947-PLAN

VISA   MasterCard   AMERICAN EXPRESS Cards   DISCOVER NOVUS

design basics inc.
HOME PLAN DESIGN SERVICE

GS1552-20 Landon
PRICE CODE

Gold Seal™
HOME PLANS

▶ **High quality, erasable, reproducible vellums**
▶ **Shipped via 2nd day air within the continental U.S.**

- volume entry expands into unique staircase
- showcase dining room with bayed window and hutch space
- French doors into den or optional guest bedroom

- efficient kitchen with corner windows
- strategically located bath
- naturally lit staircase leading to a loft with plant shelf overlooks entry area
- secondary bedrooms share a skylit bath

- large master bedroom with tiered ceiling
- arched window above whirlpool tub in beautiful master bath
- laundry room with sink conveniently located on second level

Rear Elevation

PROMOTIONAL LICENSE • PROMOTIONAL LICENSE •

Black and White, Camera-Ready Artwork of the home plan FREE with any plan purchase to assist you in advertising the home.

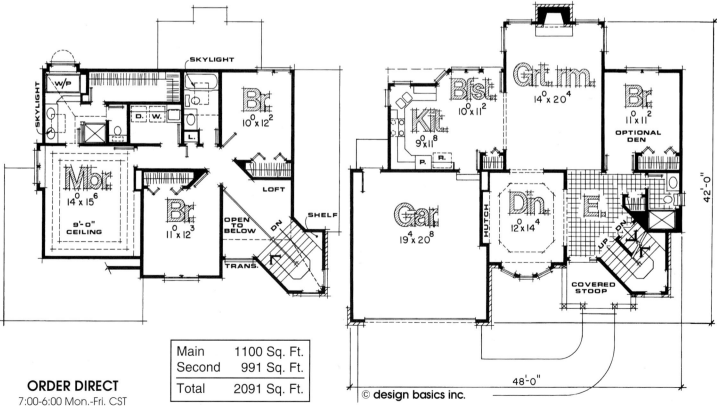

Main	1100 Sq. Ft.
Second	991 Sq. Ft.
Total	2091 Sq. Ft.

© design basics inc.

48'-0"

design basics inc.®
HOME PLAN DESIGN SERVICE

PRICE CODE

GS2156-20 Graham

▶ **High quality, erasable, reproducible vellums**
▶ **Shipped via 2nd day air within the continental U.S.**

- quaint front porch
- formal living room with 10-foot ceiling seen from entry
- dining room open to living room for entertaining options

- snack bar, pantry and window above sink in kitchen
- dinette open to informal family room for comfortable gathering
- step down into sunken family room with fireplace and windows out the back

- beautiful arched window and volume ceiling for bedroom #2
- secondary bedrooms share skylit hall bath
- private master suite with tiered ceiling and walk-in closet features angled whirlpool under window

Rear Elevation

Version of GS2100-18 the "Fenton" as seen on page 72, GS2154-19 the "Galvin" as seen on page 89 and GS2157-23 the "Lauderdale" as seen on page 76 of Homes of Elegance.

ALL PLANS *Customizable*

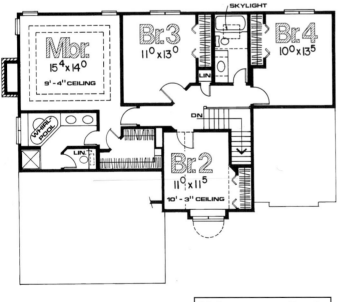

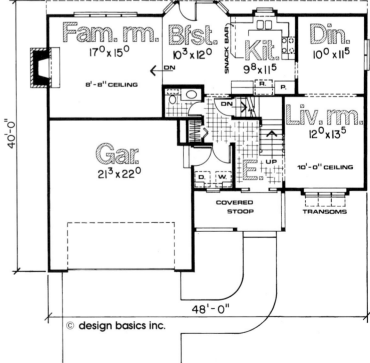

© **design basics inc.**

Main	1042 Sq. Ft.
Second	1051 Sq. Ft.
Total	2093 Sq. Ft.

ORDER DIRECT
7:00-6:00 Mon.-Fri. CST
800-947-PLAN

design basics inc.®
HOME PLAN DESIGN SERVICE

GS3209-20 Foresman

PRICE CODE **20**

▶ High quality, erasable, reproducible vellums
▶ Shipped via 2nd day air within the continental U.S.

- large covered porch is attractive feature for this 2-story
- great room off entry is warmed by fireplace
- formal dining, with interesting ceiling detail, is located near kitchen

- French doors open to well-organized peninsula kitchen with snack bar
- breakfast area provides pantries, desk area and convenient access to powder and laundry rooms

- built-in work bench in garage is added benefit
- master suite features large walk-in closet, sloped ceiling in dressing area, dual lavs, linen cabinet and whirlpool
- nice-sized bedrooms share hall bath

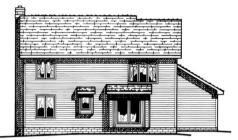

Rear Elevation

Version of GS3103-17 the "Ashworth" as seen on page 74 of Homes of Distinction.

Parade Home Package
available for all plans

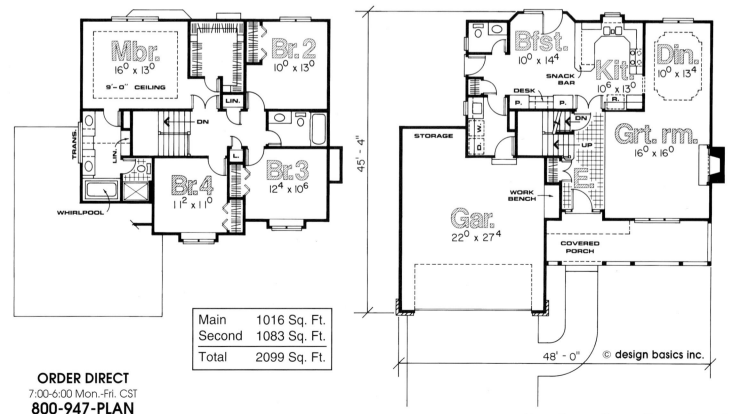

Main	1016 Sq. Ft.
Second	1083 Sq. Ft.
Total	2099 Sq. Ft.

© design basics inc.

ORDER DIRECT
7:00-6:00 Mon.-Fri. CST
800-947-PLAN

VISA MasterCard AMERICAN EXPRESS Cards DISCOVER NOVUS

design basics inc. ®
HOME PLAN DESIGN SERVICE

GS2638-21 Linden

▸ **High quality, erasable, reproducible vellums**
▸ **Shipped via 2nd day air within the continental U.S.**

- covered porch invites you into this country style home
- handsome bookcases frame fireplace in spacious family room
- double doors off entry provide family room added privacy

- kitchen features island, lazy Susan and easy access to walk-in laundry
- master bedroom features boxed ceiling and separate entries into walk-in closet and master bath

- spacious master bath features 2 lavs, whirlpool and shower
- upstairs, hall bath is compartmentalized, allowing maximum usage for today's busy families

Rear Elevation

Version of GS2648-19 the "Cyprus" as seen on page 85.

PROMOTIONAL LICENSE • Black and White, Camera-Ready Artwork of the home plan FREE with any plan purchase to assist you in advertising the home.

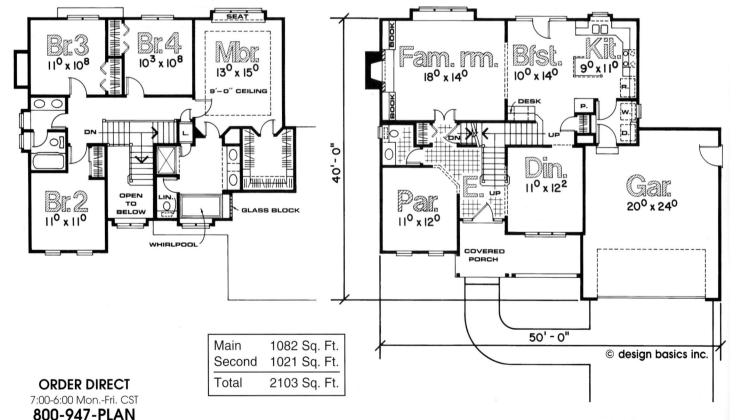

© design basics inc.

Main	1082 Sq. Ft.
Second	1021 Sq. Ft.
Total	2103 Sq. Ft.

ORDER DIRECT
7:00-6:00 Mon.-Fri. CST
800-947-PLAN

design basics inc.
HOME PLAN DESIGN SERVICE

GS826-21 Victoria

▶ **High quality, erasable, reproducible vellums**
▶ **Shipped via 2nd day air within the continental U.S.**

- dining room with hutch space and views to the outside through charming double-hung windows
- handsome wood railing separates large family room with fireplace from breakfast area

- efficient kitchen includes corner sink, pantry, island counter and breakfast area with access to the outside
- coat closet convenient to main and service entries

- master suite includes vaulted ceiling, 2 walk-in closets and double vanity
- third and fourth bedrooms offer private walk-in closets
- secondary bedrooms share central hall bath with 10-foot ceiling

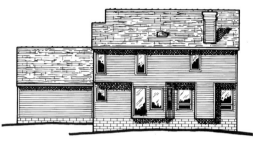

Rear Elevation

Version of GS865-21 the "Townshend" as seen on page 107.

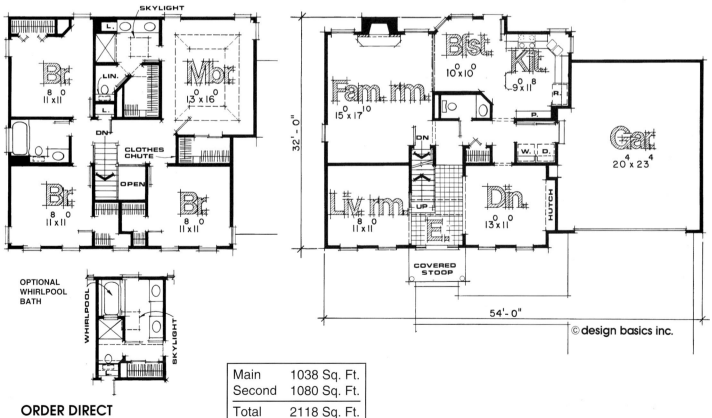

© design basics inc.

OPTIONAL WHIRLPOOL BATH

Main	1038 Sq. Ft.
Second	1080 Sq. Ft.
Total	2118 Sq. Ft.

ORDER DIRECT
7:00-6:00 Mon.-Fri. CST
800-947-PLAN

105

HOME PLAN DESIGN SERVICE

GS2618-21 Paisley

PRICE CODE

▶ **High quality, erasable, reproducible vellums**
▶ **Shipped via 2nd day air within the continental U.S.**

- beautifully proportioned design is complemented by large covered porch framed with wood railing
- living room is enhanced by warmth of a bayed window and double French doors opening to family room

- spacious dining room is accented by built-in curio cabinet
- efficient kitchen is just steps away from dinette and dining room
- family room is perfect for informal gatherings

- laundry room is conveniently accessible from kitchen, garage and directly outside
- storage space abounds in garage area
- double doors open to luxurious master bedroom with distinctive vaulted ceiling

Rear Elevation

Version of GS2619-19 the "Oakbrook" as seen on page 90.

Parade Home Package
available for all plans

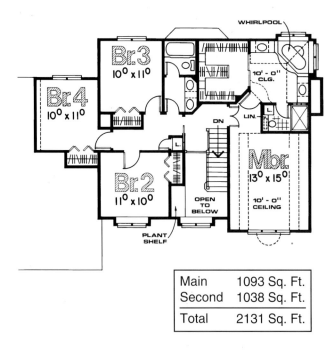

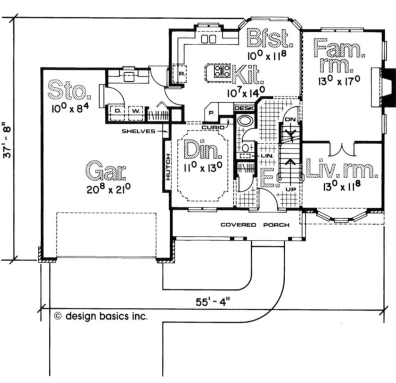

Main	1093 Sq. Ft.
Second	1038 Sq. Ft.
Total	2131 Sq. Ft.

© design basics inc.

ORDER DIRECT
7:00-6:00 Mon.-Fri. CST
800-947-PLAN

design basics inc.®
HOME PLAN DESIGN SERVICE

PRICE CODE

GS865-21 Townshend

▶ High quality, erasable, reproducible vellums
▶ Shipped via 2nd day air within the continental U.S.

- stone arch covered stoop adds old-world charm to front elevation
- entry flanked by formal entertaining rooms
- family room with fireplace secluded from entry

- island kitchen includes pantry and corner sink with windows
- laundry room also serves as mud entrance from garage
- centrally located powder bath

- master bedroom with vaulted ceiling and walk-in closet with mirrored bi-pass doors
- master dressing/bath area features sloped ceiling, skylight, double vanity and walk-in closet

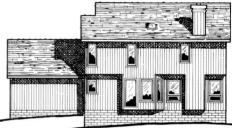

Rear Elevation

Version of GS826-21 the "Victoria" as seen on page 105.

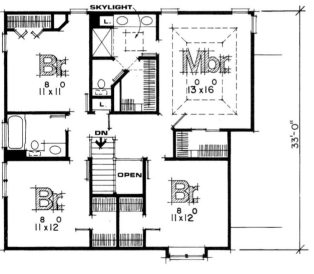

OPTIONAL WHIRLPOOL BATH

© design basics inc.

ORDER DIRECT
7:00-6:00 Mon.-Fri. CST
800-947-PLAN

Main	1038	SQ. FT.
Second	1112	SQ. FT.
Total	2150	SQ. FT.

design basics inc.®
HOME PLAN DESIGN SERVICE

Gold Seal ™
HOME PLANS

▶ **High quality, erasable, reproducible vellums**
▶ **Shipped via 2nd day air within the continental U.S.**

- covered porch and gabled roof add country feeling to this elevation
- dining room and volume parlor open to 14-foot-high entry
- French doors between parlor and family room provide space for entertaining

- family room has built-in bookcase and cased opening to dinette
- island kitchen features corner sink, large pantry, built-in bookcase and snack bar
- utility area has laundry room with sink and access from side yard and garage

- upstairs secondary bedrooms have private access to compartmented bath
- built-in dresser between his and her walk-in closets and spacious whirlpool bath add flare to master suite

P. GERNANDT

Rear Elevation

Version of plan GS2898-24 the "Lawler" as seen on page 104 of Homes of Elegance and GS2899-26 the "Bradley" as seen on page 63 of Homes of Prominence.

ALL PLANS *Customizable*

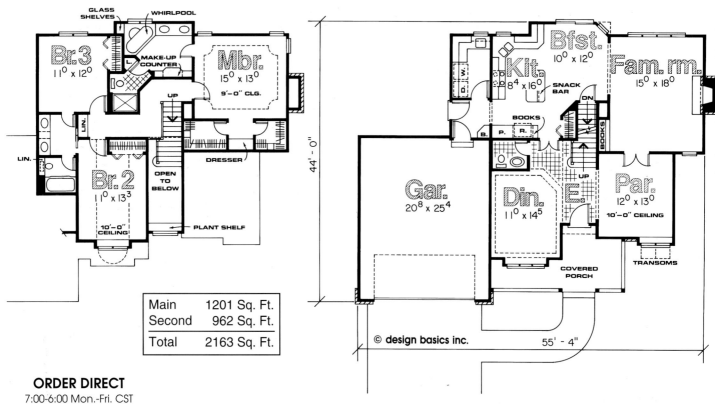

© design basics inc.

Main	1201 Sq. Ft.
Second	962 Sq. Ft.
Total	2163 Sq. Ft.

ORDER DIRECT
7:00-6:00 Mon.-Fri. CST
800-947-PLAN

design basics inc.®
HOME PLAN DESIGN SERVICE

PRICE CODE

GS2216-**21** Collier

▶ High quality, erasable, reproducible vellums
▶ Shipped via 2nd day air within the continental U.S.

Gold Seal
HOME PLANS ™

- inviting covered porch
- entry open to formal living room with volume ceiling
- abundant windows throughout
- dining room open to living room for versatility

- step down into comfortable family room with fireplace
- den with bookcase can easily open up to family room with French doors if desired
- pantry and desk in kitchen open to bayed dinette

- upstairs, bedroom #2 offers volume ceiling and half-round window
- skylit hall bath
- private master suite features plant shelf, whirlpool, skylight above vanity and walk-in closet

S. Janicek

Rear Elevation

ALL DESIGN BASICS PLANS HAVE BEEN REGISTERED
ORIGINAL C DRAFT
WITH THE U.S. COPYRIGHT OFFICE

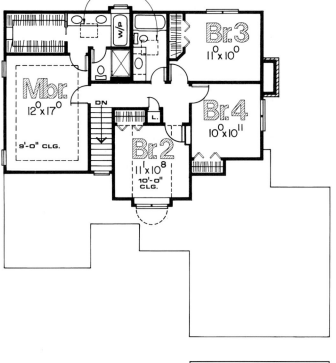

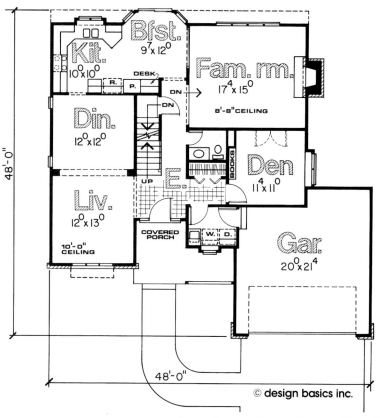

ORDER DIRECT
7:00-6:00 Mon.-Fri. CST

800-947-PLAN

VISA | MasterCard | American Express Cards | Discover Novus

Main	1224 Sq. Ft.
Second	950 Sq. Ft.
Total	2174 Sq. Ft.

© design basics inc.

design basics inc. ®
HOME PLAN DESIGN SERVICE

PRICE CODE
GS669-21 Kinston

▶ High quality, erasable, reproducible vellums
▶ Shipped via 2nd day air within the continental U.S.

Gold Seal
HOME PLANS™

- large hard-surfaced entry open to dining room
- step down to spacious great room which is visually open to breakfast area and kitchen
- central powder bath location
- airy island kitchen features a planning desk, pantry and corner sink with windows above
- bright breakfast area with many windows and access to outside
- convenient main floor laundry
- master suite enjoys window seat and volume ceiling in bedroom, double lavs, corner whirlpool, walk-in closet, plus skylight and compartmented stool and shower completing the bath area

Rear Elevation

PROMOTIONAL LICENSE

Black and White, Camera-Ready Artwork of the home plan FREE with any plan purchase to assist you in advertising the home.

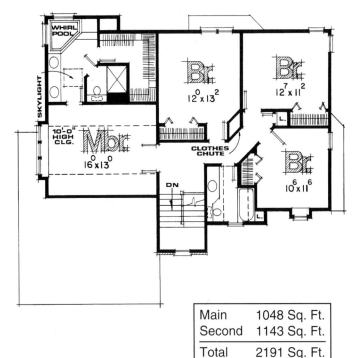

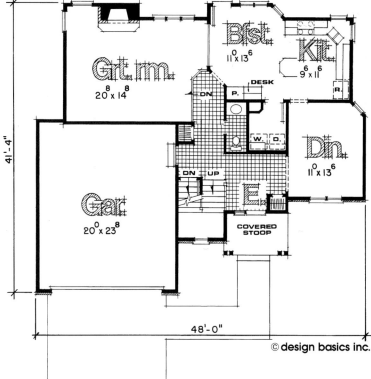

© design basics inc.

Main	1048 Sq. Ft.
Second	1143 Sq. Ft.
Total	2191 Sq. Ft.

ORDER DIRECT
7:00-6:00 Mon.-Fri. CST
800-947-PLAN

design basics inc.®
HOME PLAN DESIGN SERVICE

GS1536-21 Livingston

▶ **High quality, erasable, reproducible vellums**
▶ **Shipped via 2nd day air within the continental U.S.**

- simplified foundation
- volume living room opens to dining room with formal ceiling
- powder bath off entry
- planning desk and pantry in island kitchen

- bayed breakfast area open to family room
- step-down family room with beamed ceiling and raised hearth fireplace
- secondary bedrooms share hall bath
- efficient second level laundry

- large master bedroom with vaulted ceiling and corner windows
- luxurious master bath with window over corner whirlpool, walk-in closet, double vanity and compartmented stool and shower

Rear Elevation

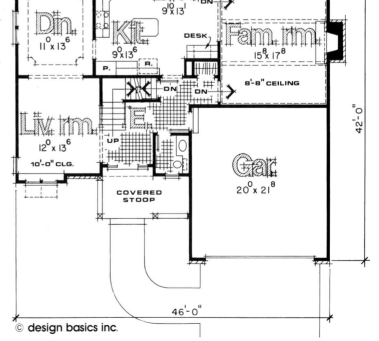

© design basics inc.

Main	1098 Sq. Ft.
Second	1095 Sq. Ft.
Total	2193 Sq. Ft.

ORDER DIRECT
7:00-6:00 Mon.-Fri. CST
800-947-PLAN

design basics inc. ®
HOME PLAN DESIGN SERVICE

PRICE CODE

GS3588-21 Stratman

- notable windows offer insight into home
- living room decorated with arched window and volume ceiling
- dining room leads to kitchen through French doors

- wet bar, fireplace and beautiful windows in casual family room
- bayed breakfast area accesses back
- kitchen includes island counter and two lazy Susans

- soaking sink in laundry room
- master suite has 9'-0" ceiling, skylight and whirlpool tub with separate shower
- room for expansion on second floor

Rear Elevation

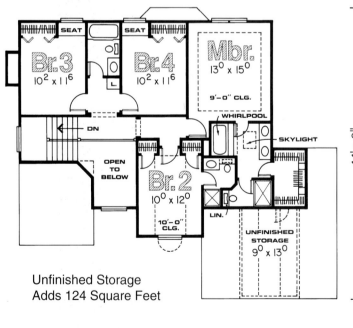

Unfinished Storage
Adds 124 Square Feet

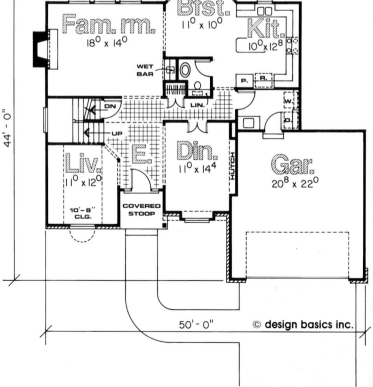

50' - 0"

© design basics inc.

Main	1179 Sq. Ft.
Second	1019 Sq. Ft.
Total	2198 Sq. Ft.

design basics inc.
HOME PLAN DESIGN SERVICE

MULTI-LEVEL HOMES

GS2457-19 Sherwood

PRICE CODE

▶ **High quality, erasable, reproducible vellums**
▶ **Shipped via 2nd day air within the continental U.S.**

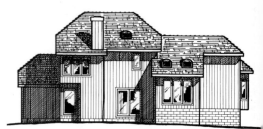

Gold Seal ™
HOME PLANS

- covered porch and window detailing adds enticement to elevation
- living room with lovely boxed ceiling open to dining room with angled windows enhances entertaining pursuits
- garage includes extra storage space

- kitchen and sunny dinette has two skylights, lots of counter space, lazy Susan and pantry
- family room offers cozy raised hearth fireplace, access to outside and large corner windows

- upstairs, secondary bedrooms share convenient hall bath
- comfortable master bedroom features vaulted ceiling and two closets
- skylit compartmented master bath with decorative plant shelf

Rear Elevation

PROMOTIONAL LICENSE • PROMOTIONAL LICENSE

Black and White, Camera-Ready Artwork of the home plan FREE with any plan purchase to assist you in advertising the home.

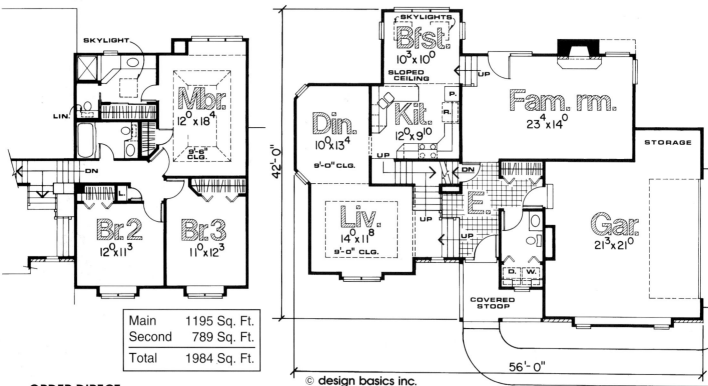

Main	1195 Sq. Ft.
Second	789 Sq. Ft.
Total	1984 Sq. Ft.

© design basics inc.

ORDER DIRECT

7:00-6:00 Mon.-Fri. CST
800-947-PLAN

design basics inc.®
HOME PLAN DESIGN SERVICE

PRICE CODE

GS2456-19 Santa Rosa

- ▶ High quality, erasable, reproducible vellums
- ▶ Shipped via 2nd day air within the continental U.S.

Gold Seal HOME PLANS ™

- brick and lap siding combination gives appeal to elevation
- inviting entry views great room and dining room
- spacious great room features raised hearth fireplace and sunny windows

- kitchen and dinette area has outdoor access, wrapping counters, two lazy Susans, built-in desk and snack bar
- unfinished family room, half-bath and laundry facilitate future expansion

- three comfortable secondary bedrooms upstairs
- upstairs, master suite has vaulted ceiling and pampering compartmented bath and dressing area with whirlpool, huge walk-in closet and dual lavs

Rear Elevation

ALL PLANS *Customizable*

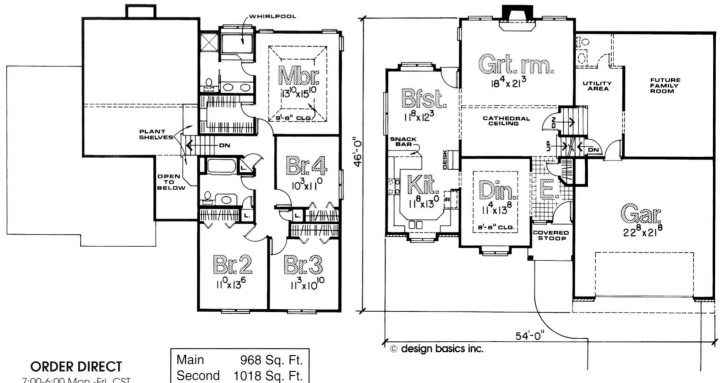

© design basics inc.

ORDER DIRECT
7:00-6:00 Mon.-Fri. CST
800-947-PLAN

Main	968 Sq. Ft.
Second	1018 Sq. Ft.
Total	1986 Sq. Ft.

design basics inc. ®
HOME PLAN DESIGN SERVICE

ORDERING INFORMATION

Name _____   Company _____

Address _____   Title _____
(Packages cannot be shipped to a P.O. Box)

Above Address ☐ business ☐ residence   City _____ State ____ Zip _____

☐ VISA **VISA**   ☐ AMEX   Phone (____) _____

☐ MasterCard **MasterCard**   ☐ Discover **DISCOVER**   FAX (____) _____

Credit Card ☐☐☐☐☐☐☐☐☐☐☐☐☐☐   Exp. Date _____

All COD's must be paid by Certified Check, Cashier's Check or Money Order.
(Additional $5.00 charge on COD orders)

PLAN PRICES SUBJECT TO CHANGE   Signature _____

PLAN NUMBER	PLAN NAME	AMOUNT
GS2578	The Kaiser	$495.00
Additional sets of prints with plan purchase Quantity: ___ @ ea. $10.00		
	SUBTOTAL	

PRODUCT CODE	PLAN NUMBER	DESCRIPTION	QTY.	AMOUNT
MEW	GS2578	Materials and Estimator's Workbook	1	$50.00

BOOK NUMBER	QTY.	AMOUNT

CANADIAN BLUEPRINTS
1969 — 1999
ORDER HOTLINE
1-800-561-4169
30th YEAR

SHIPPING & HANDLING	
(CONTINENTAL U.S.)	

Home Plans			Books & Products	
2nd Bus. Day	n/c		UPS Ground (4-5 bus.days)	$4.95
Next Bus. Day	$15.00		2nd Business Day	$10.00
			Next Business Day	$20.00
SAME DAY SHIPPING IF			Any Single Plan Book	$2.95
ORDERED BY 2:00 P.M. C.T.			Any Combination of Plan Books	$4.95

SUBTOTAL OF PLANS, PRODUCTS AND BOOKS	
NE Res. add 6.5% Tax	
SHIPPING & HANDLING (see chart at left)	
TOTAL	

FOR FASTEST SERVICE, CALL
800-947-7526
MONDAY-FRIDAY,
7:00 A.M. TO 6:00 P.M. C.T.
OR FAX
(402) 331-5507
DESIGN BASICS INC.
11112 John Galt Blvd.
Omaha, NE 68137-2384

Visit us on the Internet
http://www.designbasics.com
E-Mail: dbi @ synergy.net

— Home Plan Price Schedule —

Plan Price Code	Total Square Feet	1 Set Master Vellums
18	1800-1899	$515
19	1900-1999	$525
20	2000-2099	$535
21	2100-2199	$545

No refunds or exchanges, please. All orders are payable in U.S. funds only.
All Design Basics home plans come with a basement foundation. Home plans do not carry an architect's/engineer's stamp.
You may need to obtain an architect's/engineer's stamp to comply with your local building codes.

Available for any Gold Seal™ plan, our economical **Parade Home Package (A,B,C),** includes (A) Cus-

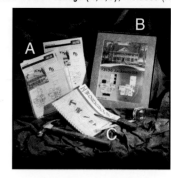

tomized Promotional Handout Artwork, (B) a Full-Color Rendering, and (C) the Materials and Estimator's Workbook, along with an acrylic literature holder, great for displaying your Promotional Handout copies.

Only $149 (#PHP).

A. Our **Customized Promotional Handout Artwork** is a favorite sales tool among home builders nationwide. Each camera-ready, 8½" x 11" master copy comes ready for reproduction, with your name, address, telephone number and even company logo, if desired. Available for all Gold Seal™ plans.

Only $69 (#PHA).

B. Display a dream with our 11" x 14" Gold Seal™ **Color Renderings.** Each is an artist's original, hand-colored portrayal of the front elevation and floor plan of the home of your choice. Mounted in a 13" x 16" black metal frame, with a grey marble matte.

Only $99 (#CR). Unframed $79 (#CR).

C. Our **Materials and Estimator's Workbook** is designed to save valuable time in the budgeting process, ensure accurate and comparable bids and help eliminate errors. It also allows you to track projected costs vs. actual expenditures throughout the construction process. Available for each Gold Seal™ plan. Does not include slab foundation.

Only $50 (#MEW).

Specific for any Design Basics plan, our **Study Print & Furniture Layout Guide** makes it easy to visualize the finished home. Includes views of all exterior elevations plus a ¼" scale floor plan with over 100 reusable furniture pieces, a useful ¼" scale ruler and helpful tips on space planning.

Now with Clear-Backed Furniture Pieces

Only $29.95 (#SP).